W9-CLE-568

Dangling Lines

"There is always hope in a dangling line"
Norwegian proverb.

Social and Economic Studies No. 50
Institute of Social and Economic Research
Memorial University of Newfoundland

Dangling Lines

The Fisheries Crisis and the Future of Coastal Communities: The Norwegian Experience

Svein Jentoft

ISER

Institute of Social and Economic Research

© Svein Jentoft 1993
All rights reserved

Published by the
Institute of Social and Economic Research
Memorial University of Newfoundland
St. John's, Newfoundland, Canada
ISBN 0-919666-85-X

An earlier version of this book was published in Norwegian by
Ad Notam Gyldendal forlag AS, Oslo, Norway 1991.

Over 50% recycled paper
including 10% post
consumer fibre
Plus de 50 p. 100 de
papier recyclé dont 10 p.
100 de fibres post-
consommation.

∞
Printed on acid-free paper

M - Official mark of Environment Canada
M - Marque officielle d'Environnement Canada

Canadian Cataloguing in Publication Data
Jentoft, Svein, 1948-

Dangling lines

(Social and Economic Studies, ISSN 0847-0898 ;
no. 50)

Translation of: Hengende snøre.
Includes bibliographical references.
ISBN 0-919666-85-X

1. Cod-fisheries -- Norway. 2. Fishery policy --
Norway. 3. Fisheries -- Social aspects -- Norway.
I. Memorial University of Newfoundland. Institute of
Social and Economic Research. II. Title.
III. Series: Social and economic studies (St.
John's, Nfld.) ; no. 50.

SH279.J46 1993   338.3'727'09481   C93-098670-9

This book has been published with the help of a grant from the Department of Fisheries, Government of Newfoundland and Labrador.

A heated argument with the fisheries minister: Lofoten, winter, 1990.
Credit: Kurt Haugli.

Contents

To my mother and in memory of my father.

Preface

This book is about the fisheries crisis that struck Norway in 1989, the problems it created and the challenges it raised for the future. Fisheries has always been a major export industry in Norway, and it has played a crucial role in maintaining the settlement, particularly in the north. There are more than 800 fishing communities in the country and today the fishing industry employs about 25,000 fishermen (of which 98 percent are men), 10,000 fish-plant workers (50 percent are women), and 7,000 people in fish farming (30 percent women).

Crisis is not new in the Norwegian fishing industry. While the word has been used for many years however, "crisis" has never been more appropriate.

The fishing industry originated the saying: "There is hope in a dangling line!" The opportunities are there, the persistent ones will be rewarded. However, a wait-and-see attitude does not work. The hope will not be realized unless something is ventured. In present day coastal Norway and in the fishing industry in particular, there is much to be done. And time is running out.

That is the basis of this book and its theme. Much of the material in it originated from research projects in which I have been involved in recent years. Some of the projects were undertaken on behalf of the Coastal Expertise Committee (Kystkompetanseutvalget), [1] which presented its position in May 1990. Other projects were carried out with the support of the Norwegian Fisheries Research Council (Norges Fiskeriforskningsråd). None of the projects was started with a view to examining the effects of the coastal crisis in particular. They are nevertheless useful in pointing to a way out of the crisis.

The coastal crisis has been the subject of discussion with many of my close colleagues. Without them this book would not have seen the light of day. Jacob Meløe and Viggo Rossvær must be particularly mentioned. Many of the projects were carried out in cooperation with others. I would like to thank Trond Kristoffersen, Petter Holm, Bardon Steene, Marit Husmo, Anne Hjortdal, Jan Trollvik, Johnny Didriksen, Alf Håkon Hoel, Ernst Bolle, Eva Munk-Madsen, Victor Thiessen and Anthony Davis. Inspiration also came from conversations with Abraham Hallenstvedt, Aslak Kristiansen, Trond Wold, Anita Maurstad, Ottar Brox, Helge O. Larsen, Harald Normann, Hans Ludvik Myhra, Cato Wadel, Bjørn Hersoug and Bonnie McCay. Useful comments which helped to improve the manuscript were provided by Greta Jentoft, Knut Mikalsen, Håkan Sandersen and Kjell Arne Røvik. A special thank you must also be extended to Iens Ludvig Høst who employed me as researcher for the Coastal Expertise Committee. NORAS (Norwegian Council for Applied Social Research) helped fund the publishing

Preface to the English Edition

The publication of this book in Canada is in good part due to my friends Berit and Victor R. Pittman. Not only have they translated the text from Norwegian to English, but the idea of actually writing this book in the first place had its inception during a visit to their home at Head of St. Margaret's Bay, Halifax County, Nova Scotia, during the summer of 1990. I am very grateful to them.

In the English version I have added three new chapters—Chapters 2, 14 and 16, on the advice of the editor of ISER Books, Robert Paine. His constructive suggestions were very helpful. Also I am grateful to Richard Apostle for pointing out things in the manuscript that needed clarification for Canadian readers.

Oddmund Otterstad helped prepare the map of the fishing municipalities included in this book. Martin Arne Andersen helped me acquire the statistics on the effects of the fisheries crisis. Geir Runar Karlsen helped me to make the index. In addition, Bjørn Tore Forberg, journalist for the newspaper *Fiskeribladet*, kindly gave me access to his large collection of photographs. All photographs with one exception were provided by him. I am very grateful for all the assistance I received.

The Norwegian Research Council—Social Science section, (Norges Forskningsråds, avd. Rådet for Samfunnsforskning) and Norut Samfunn A/S helped fund the translation.

In the preparation of this English edition much is owed to Susan Nichol and Jeanette Gleeson of the ISER Books team. Thank you.

Tromsø, May 1993   Svein Jentoft

Map 1. Norway and Newfoundland.

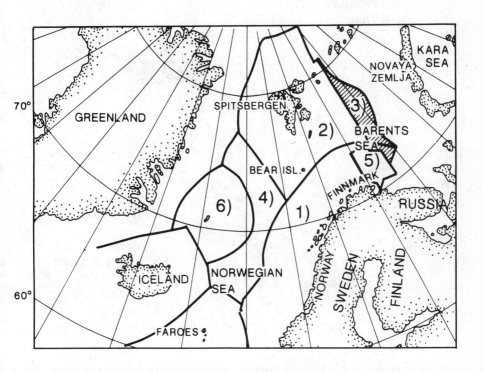

1 Norwegian Economic Zone—200 mile
2 The Spitsbergen Fishery Conservation Zone (Norwegian responsibility)
3 "The Loophole" (International waters)
4 Norwegian Sea "Loophole" (International waters)
5 "The Grey Zone": Interim fishery conservation regime
6 The Jan Mayen Fishery Conservation Zone (Norwegian Area)

Map 2. Norwegian fishing zones

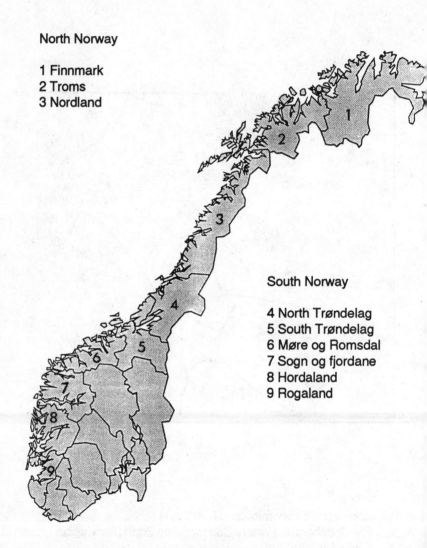

North Norway

1 Finnmark
2 Troms
3 Nordland

South Norway

4 North Trøndelag
5 South Trøndelag
6 Møre og Romsdal
7 Sogn og fjordane
8 Hordaland
9 Rogaland

Map 3. Norwegian fishing provinces.

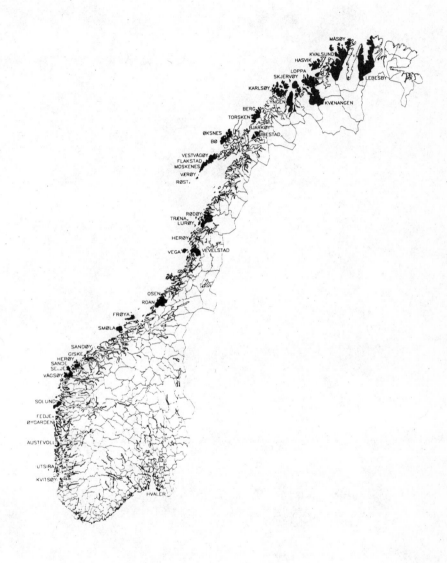

Map 4. Norwegian fishing municipalities.

Introduction
Long Live the Coast?

The bomb dropped during the first days of October 1989. The cod stocks in the Barents Sea were at an historical low. "Drastic cuts in fishing quotas are unavoidable," said the oceanographic researchers when they returned from their fall inspection. The news created a furore. People along the coast reacted with "shock, anger, doubt and disbelief—but little hope," the newspaper *Nordlys* reported on 6 October. After years of low quotas, they thought that bottom had been struck and that it would now be possible to harvest the fruits of the strict regulations that had been in force. Some years previously, the scientists had predicted that it should be possible to catch 900,000 tonnes in 1990. Instead, a notice was now issued that the quotas for 1990 and for many years to come would be slashed to 100,000 tonnes. The Minister of Fisheries was surprised, and so was the Director of Fisheries. The quota estimates surprised everyone, not least the researchers themselves. The disappointment was almost palpable and the fishermen considered themselves cheated. After some time, a decision was made to let the Norwegian fishermen take 113,000 tonnes, less than a third of what they had been allowed to catch a few years earlier. Such low cod quotas could not be offset by fishing for other species. "A fishery without cod is no fishery at all," commented Arvid Hylen, Chief of Research at the Oceanographic Research Institute. The coastal crisis was upon us.

OVER THE EDGE

In the days that followed, the newspapers used their blackest headlines: "Coastal Norway in shock" (*Nordlys*); "The coast is now experiencing a downright catastrophe which the authorities can't understand" (*Fiskeribladet*); "Finnmark falls overboard" (*Finnmark Dagblad*); "Over the edge" (*Lofotposten*). Even politicians spoke in dramatic terms. "The word 'crisis' does not adequately describe the environmental tragedy we are faced with today," member of Parliament Karl Erik Schjøtt Pedersen told a press conference.

There was no end of suggestions for solving the problem. The fisheries crisis filled column after column in the coastal press. "Stop the Lofoten fisheries!" said the Troms county branch of the Norwegian Fishermen's Association (Troms Fiskarfylking).[1] "Close the Barents Sea!" said the Provincial Legislature of Nordland. The Troms Labour Party was in favour of halting the trawler fishery in the Barents Sea for the rest of the decade. *Sunnmøre Fiskarlag* disputed the oceanographic researchers' recommendations and suggested doubling the cod quota. "The (Norwegian) factory trawlers must leave the Norwegian zone," said Rudolf Johannesen, chairman of Nordland Province Fishermen's Association (Nordland Fylkesfiskarlag). The Minister of Fisheries, Bjarne Mørk Eidem, expressed similar sentiments. Representatives of the trawler industry resented being singled out as the principal villains. They felt the trawlers should be given priority when allocating cod quotas for 1990 and they justified this by pointing to the importance of the fleet to the fish processing industry. They also suggested that if one is looking for a villain then one should look to the neighbour to the east. The Soviet Ambassador dismissed the inference that the Russians were responsible for the resource crisis and was supported by the Chief of the Norwegian Coast Guard who said that the Russian trawlers, by and large, have adhered to the regulations.

The debate about the fisheries crisis quickly developed into a traditional north-south conflict. "The fisheries crisis is primarily a North Norway problem," wrote Svein Krane director of the National Association of the Fish Processing Industry in the organization's magazine. Many shared that opinion and felt that the authorities should take the blame. "Reserve the cod in the north for the fishermen in the north," was a frequently heard demand, not least from Finnmark. Svenn Tore Olsen, representative of the Seamen's Association, believed such a suggestion would lead to "conditions of civil war." In South Norway warnings were issued against considering the crisis solely a North Norway matter and it was pointed out that the coastal societies of Trøndelag and Vestlandet are also affected. From the north and the south, people maintained that the crisis was more a conflict between the inshore fleet and the deep-sea fleet than between Vestlandet and North Norway. The fishermen in Sogn and Fjordane, for example, demanded "management which pays less attention to capital and more to people" (*Fiskeribladet* 13 February 1990).

THE COAST IN REVOLT

Meetings and conferences were held in the municipalities and provinces and in the industrial organizations. Resolutions were adopted and protests written. New actors entered the debate. The Nature Conservancy Association of Norway achieved observer status on the Regulation Board. The Saami Parliament emphasized that the coastal Saami have special rights which must be considered in fisheries regulations, and they were supported by members of the legal community. At Sørøya in Finnmark, the women organized themselves under the leadership of Hanne Nilsen, and reminded everyone that it is not only boats and companies that are affected, but also families, women and children. Doctors came forward, warning about health-related consequences of the crisis, and that the whole coastal society in North Norway would need crisis psychiatry.

Even the Board of the University of Tromsø commented on the crisis: "Not only the value of the ocean resources but also the values of our culture are in danger." From the pulpit, sermons were preached about the catastrophe which hit the coast. The Chief of Defence for North Norway was concerned. Per Borten, Hanna Kvanmo and other well-known public personalities demanded, in letters to the Government, that a separate commission be set up to look into the management of the fisheries. For the first time, the three provincial legislatures in North Norway met to discuss the crisis.

On 14 December, an historical first extraordinary national meeting was called by the Fishermen's Association of Norway (Norges Fiskarlag). The delegates wanted answers to the question: "Don't they expect people to live along the coast?"

If the fishermen were not already aware of the situation they were in, it became clear to them when the Christmas holidays ended and the allocation of quotas was ready. "For the first time, the year begins with a moratorium on the fisheries," wrote *Nordlys.* "In beautiful winter weather, January 2 should have been a fine day to begin the winter fisheries, but on Sommarøya the mood on the shore is darker than the ocean outside."

On January 9, the town of Ålesund organized its own coastal fisheries action and protest letters were sent to the authorities. Their action was applauded by the fishermen from north to south. "The coast in revolt," wrote *Fiskeribladet* on January 16, 1990. The debate included some strong language. Even the Minister of Fisheries, Svein Munkejord, was drawn into a duel of harsh words and had to explain to the Prime Minister an incident that took place over a glass of beer in a pub in Tromsø.[2] On January 28, the first nation-wide general strike since 1936 was held. Appeals for support and national solidarity went out. "Help is needed to prevent the fishermen from losing house and home," said the chairman of the Troms county branch of the Norwegian Fishermen's Association. It is important to "have a warm heart and a cool head," noted Thor Robertsen, provincial councillor for Finnmark. Leiv Grønnevedt, secretary general of the Fishing Boat Owners Association (Fiskebåtredernes Forbund) said that "four to five thousand businesses and a total of 40,000 jobs are at stake. The populations of 500 to 700 local settlements are in jeopardy. A complete small-industry culture is at risk." A research report from the Norwegian Institute for Town and Regional Research estimated that Coastal Norway will lose 8,000 man-years in 1990. Despite the letters and declarations, some people in the fisheries felt isolated in their plight. "I wonder whether anyone cares about what is now happening to us in Coastal Norway, other than those of us who are in the middle of it all," a fisherman's wife said in a letter to the editor of *Fiskeribladet*.

AWARENESS

Even though the greatest waves have subsided, the debate continues. Little by little, the long-term and critical questions have been brought into sharper focus. Many of these problems had not been discussed much before the crisis (at least the crisis had the positive effect of stimulating new discussion). How should the fisheries be regulated in the future so that we don't end up in the same situation again? What does it mean, in concrete terms, to venture on a coastal policy which seriously aims at "sustainable development"? These are important questions which need to be investigated.

   In the course of the past four years, since the oceanographic researchers published their report on the cod stock in the Barents Sea, people have come to realize that we have a coastal culture worth preserving. It is not only the livelihood of people which is at stake. A special way of life, a way of life which has unique traditions and qualities, is also in danger. Such perspectives are new in the fisheries policy debate in Norway. They have initiated discussion about the rights of coastal people, about whether the fisheries should continue to be open to all and whether the commons should be privatized or regionalized. Such principles, among others, were discussed in January, 1991, at a conference arranged by the University of Tromsø, in cooperation with the Regional Committee (Landsdelsutvalget) for North Norway and Namdalen, under the title: "The Right to the Fish Resources." It is unusual for a conference with such a theme to be held in Norway.

At the same time, the cod crisis has focused more attention on the financial benefits created by the fishing industry. When there is a shortage, the question is raised as to whether we utilize the resources properly. What can be done, for example, to improve the quality of fish products so that we can get a better market price for them? How can we make our firms more knowledgeable to meet this challenge? Do we have to change our legislation to achieve this?

Little by little, the authorities also began to participate more actively. A special Coastal Report was presented during the spring of 1991. It was called "cold mush" by the newspaper *Dagens Næringsliv*, but there is no doubt that the report heeded the debate which followed in the wake of the fisheries crisis. Not all suggestions were received equally well by everyone. For example, the proposal to decentralize management responsibility, that is, to pass it on to the provinces,[3] and to exert better control over the regional distribution of fish quotas, met with widespread opposition.

Warnings have now been issued that radical measures must be taken to reduce the overcapacity of the fishing fleet by establishing a system of transferable quotas. It was also announced that the Raw Fish Act needed revision. Just before the summer recess in 1991, Parliament adopted measures to ease the requirement that fish-farming plants be locally owned. These proposals provoked strong reactions, not least in North Norway, where many fear a precedent will be set for taking away regional control of resources, putting the area in worse straits than ever. "Can we trust our own politicians?" asked novelist Hans Kristian Eriksen, whose view is that North Norwegian politicians are "regional traitors" who would lay waste this region of the country (*Nordlys* 26 June 1991).

SOCIAL SCIENTISTS NEEDED

At the height of the debate over the fisheries crisis in the fall of 1989, many people wondered about the social scientists. Where were they? Had they nothing to contribute? Did their "deafening silence" reveal a lack of involvement or lack of knowledge, or both? Many of us felt hurt by these suggestions. It took some time, that is true, before we got on track. We were as much in shock as everybody else; we, too, had assumed that the previously positive prognosis issued by the oceanographic researchers was accurate. We needed some time to review what we could contribute professionally to the new situation, and little by little, our ideas appeared in newspapers and at conferences. A review of newspapers two years later shows that social scientists did, indeed, leave their mark on the debate.

This book is a summary and a further development of my own contribution to the discussion of the coastal crisis. Not all problems raised by the crisis are examined here. Many of my colleagues have brought up important matters which I recognize are relevant but which I have not touched on, either because I have nothing to add or because I do not feel competent to comment on them. I have therefore left such matters to others.

CONTENTS OF BOOK

This book covers a wide variety of topics which I have researched for many years, even before the crisis occurred. The manner in which the fisheries are regulated is dealt with in Chapters 3, 10, 13 and 15. That the regulation of the fisheries is the key problem whenever the crisis is discussed is evident from the debates referred to above; whoever is looking for a solution to the coastal problems should start there.

The challenges in the fish processing industry in this age of bio- and computer technology are the focus of Chapters 4, 5 and 6. Fish processing is a traditional industry, but it is in the process of acquiring the most modern technology. This requires a radical upgrading of technical expertise in the plants. It also raises the question of which forms of organization should be developed locally in the fishing industry.

How the fisheries crisis has been experienced by the people along the coast, and the social and economic consequences that can be traced in the official statistics are the themes of Chapter 2. The situation of women in the fishing districts is analyzed in Chapters 7, 8 and 9. A fishing society which does not function satisfactorily for both sexes is doomed. The fisheries policy is faced with an enormous challenge here.

There are great expectations that new industries will improve the situation in the coastal municipalities. Fish farming shows formidable growth and the prognosis for the future is promising. However, the fish farming industry is at present facing hard times and there are doubts about whether it will continue to play the role of a district industry as effectively as was envisaged. Tourism is another economic possibility for some coastal districts. The coast can offer unique natural and cultural experiences if these assets are maintained. Efforts must be made to ensure that the "authentic" coastal culture is not lost. Fish farming and tourism are analyzed in Chapters 10 and 11.

Low technical expertise can make the future look threatening instead of challenging. The fisheries-dependent coastal communities have a particularly weak base and a lot could be done to raise levels of expertise. It is not only at the local level, however, that more knowledge is required; some maintain that the fisheries crisis is a manifestation of organizational and management problems in the fishing industry and fisheries management. LOM (Leadership, Organization and Management) is one of our national fields of research. This type of research should also focus on problems along our coast. In Chapter 12, I question the knowledge on which the fisheries policy is based and indicate where there is a need for LOM-directed research.

Chapter 15 of this book deals with fisheries policy. The developments which culminated in the crisis now being experienced on the coast demand drastic measures. I ask: is it possible to agree on a governing principle for the management of our fisheries resources? Are the politicians capable of making the necessary choices to ensure that the coast survives? Is there, realistically, any hope in a dangling line?

Much has happened since the crisis first broke and many things have changed. Chapter 16 updates the situation and poses the question: what can we learn from the fisheries crisis?

I have used, and will continue to use, the terms cod crisis, fisheries crisis and coastal crisis interchangeably. This mixture is more than a linguistic variation. One crisis leads to another which results in a third. This is how it has always been and always will be. If you doubt what the social scientists are saying, then read Petter Dass, and his ode to Northern Norway.

> If Codfish forsake us, what then would we hold?
> What carry to Bergen to barter for gold?
> Our boats would ride high in the water...
>
> Aye, Fish in the water, that's our Daily Bread
> And if we should lose it we'd soon be near dead
> And, heartsick, loud wail out our sorrow.[4]

Blacker than Black!   2

In June 1988 the sheriff of Vardø wrote a letter to the provincial commissioner of Finnmark: "In the ten years that I have resided in this district I have never experienced such pessimism among the population."

Finnmark, the most northerly and most fisheries-dependent province, had then endured several years of seal invasions and poor fishing. East-Finnmark, in particular, had been hit by the problem. "Vardø for sale!" wrote *Fiskeribladet* (9 June 1988), when the town experienced a dramatic increase in bankruptcies among the fishermen. Not only their vessels came under the hammer, but their homes too. Houses not up for auction were put on the market voluntarily. "Never have there been so many houses for sale in this district. The situation is quite frightening," maintained the sheriff.

Worse was yet to come. The year 1990 was the most difficult year in the history of modern Norwegian fisheries. Never had cod quotas been so low. The situation in the fisheries was "blacker than black," confirmed a fisheries guidance counsellor in North Troms in his annual report. The crisis in Finnmark spread southward along the coast and in its wake came pessimism. "One of the things we asked for in the past year has been answered. We asked that there be a stop to the slow torture of the coastal fishermen. Yes, this torture has stopped. Completely. The main artery has simply been cut," a fisherwoman commented bitterly to *Fiskeribladet* (19 January 1990).

A NEW TYPE OF POVERTY?

That winter few saw any hope in the dangling line; the crisis shook their faith in the future. One fisherman told *Lofotposten* (16 January 1990): "I dread almost every day. Will I get any bills in the mail today?

The meaning of my life has been taken away. They are not going to get my boat. Over my dead body. It is all I have. A life's work after 23 years on the sea."

Heartbreaking outbursts like these abounded in the media during 1990. The financial difficulties, the unpaid bills, and the desperation of individual fishing families were pervasive themes. "It undermines one's dignity," said Hanne Nilsen, a fisherwoman in Hasvik in Finnmark. The philosopher Viggo Rossvær at the University of Tromsø saw an existential as well as economic aspect to the pile of unpaid bills on the window sill. "It tells about people who have ended up in debt to the greater society because they want to defend the value of their way of life. People feel threatened because they want to continue to be what they were."

At a public meeting in Lofoten (attended by the Minister of Fisheries) the leader of the Coastal Fishers' Association, Steinar Friis, opened his speech:

> Today is Wednesday, 17 January, 1990. The Coastal fleet is tied up at the wharf. The fishing gear is idle. The fishermen and their families have great financial problems. They fear the coming winter, spring and fall. Next year—five years—many years. They fear notices from the bank. The sound of the auctioneer's hammer which hangs in the sheriff's office. And, most of all, they fear the authorities who, under the guise of democracy, are reducing the lifework of thousands to ruins, making the coastal people into refugees on their own soil. Honourable Minister! This is the reality for us—for the people of the coast—in the year 1990.

The crisis affected the pocketbook. Once the winter fisheries were over, the accounts were tallied at Botnhamn on Senja in Troms. *Nordlys* (23 May 1990) reported that eight to ten women employed at the community's only fish plant had their income reduced from 29,000 NOK the previous winter to 11,000 that year; the roughly thirty fishermen had earned 129,000 NOK the previous year, but only 48,000 that year. The newspaper addressed the ordinary Norwegian: "If you are crying because you received a wage increase of only 3 to 4 percent, then spare a kind thought for the people of Botnhamn and of the many other places along the coast who are now living with a wage settlement which nobody envies . . . We can see the trail leading towards a new poverty among the people and fewer and fewer see any way out of this crisis."

Similar reports came from other places. The fisheries counsellor for Røst, furthest out on the Lofoten chain of islands, stated in his annual report for 1990 that for the individual fishermen, the 1990 quota meant a reduction of 83 percent, compared to the amount caught during the winter of 1989.

COLLECTIVE DEPRESSION

The fisheries crisis brought the Public Health authorities out. The Finnmark provincial medical officer, Doctor Berit Olsen, wrote that "collective depression is the most distinctive characteristic of the health conditions in Finnmark today" (Olsen 1990). To be sure, she offers a new medical concept here, but it describes very well the mood in the local economy. According to Olsen, people exhibit both resignation and a flight from reality. "On the one hand, they describe misery which contributes to maintaining depression and which, in the worst scenario, may become a self-fulfilling prophecy; on the other hand, denial is expressed in an optimism without any basis in reality and which therefore contributes to preventing reorientation and new readjustment."

Collective depression seemed to be contagious. "The worst epidemic since the Black Death" was the conclusion at a fishermen's meeting in Hasvik municipality (*Fiskerbladet* 18 January 1990).[1] The crisis permeated the atmosphere in the local society and affected everybody regardless of whether they drew their income from the sea or not. People became discouraged not only for their own sake but on the part of others.

How to remedy such a situation? Few have a prescription. No doctor can prescribe any medicine for low cod quotas. "Economic grieving is not a disease, even if it does produce pain," Olsen pointed out; the health system cannot solve the political and social problems of the fisheries crisis. The Minister of Fisheries, Svein Munkejord, could not give many words of comfort. He attended a public meeting in Alta where a fisherwoman wondered how she and her husband would manage: "My husband has a thirty foot boat. He has been given a quota of eleven tonnes of round fish. With such a small quota we will only be able to pay the insurance on the boat. Interest and instalments will have to wait." The Minister replied: "Unfortunately I stand helpless in telling you how you and your husband will survive with such a small quota. But with the imagination which the coastal population is known to have, and hard work I am sure you will find a solution" (*Finnmark Dagblad* 8 February 1990).

Dean Jørgen Rostrup, however, had a suggestion. At a public meeting on Røst, the priest urged the people to work together: "Unless we stand together we will be reduced to zero" (*Fiskeribladet* 22 March 1990). His suggestion inspired the local mayor to encourage a special "coastal action" which gathered support along the whole coast. On Røst, they found resources in the local population which they did not know existed there: "The people of Røst have adopted a new type of community spirit," wrote *Fiskeribladet.* Even the mayor was surprised at the solidarity and unity displayed. In his annual report, the fisheries counsellor on Røst reported that this action contributed to turning the mood from deep pessimism to belief in the future.

THE EIGHT COMMANDMENTS

But Røst appears to be an exception. Reports of such morale were hard to find in 1990. Instead, personal misfortunes dominated: fishermen going bankrupt, becoming unemployed, losing house and home. Fishermen often take loans on their houses to finance their boats, and so stand to lose both. The fisherman who had been his own master and accustomed to self-sufficiency ends up on social assistance and, in the most severe cases, receives disability payments. This hurts the family, which cannot cope with a depressed husband and father who has nothing to do. Many fishing municipalities have also experienced a dramatic increase in welfare support. "The coastal crisis and the unemployment are reflected in greatly increased social assistance cases and child welfare problems," wrote the head of the Social Department for Måsøy municipality in his annual report for 1990. In Bø municipality, for example, social assistance expenses doubled in the course of 1989 and 1990 as a result of the fisheries crisis.

The fisheries crisis has also created work for the municipal health workers. In her medical report for 1990, Berit Olsen, the provincial medical officer for Finnmark reported that a questionnaire sent out to municipal doctors and general practitioners found that in one week almost 30 percent of the doctors had reported patients unfit for work and that unemployment was the contributing cause. "Almost 80 percent of the doctors see special health problems in which depression, pain, frequent back problems, sleep disorders, intoxication, sexual problems, ulcers and deterioration of the heart are the most frequent complaints." A medical survey among the fishermen in the Lofoten region found the same trend.

Dagbladet (11 October 1989) reported "an enormous increase" at the twelve crisis centres for women in North Norway, where "there are clear indications of a correlation between the fishing moratorium and family violence." The municipal medical officer in Loppa predicted, "If this meaningless stress situation continues, then there will be a considerable increase in normal diseases, depression, abuse, sexual problems and suicides" (*Fiskeribladet* 18 January

1990). He is supported by other doctors, who feel that help must come quickly.

Guri Ingebrigtsen, a psychiatrist in Lofoten suggests that fishermen are more exposed to mental stress than people in other professions, and that this is related to their having created their own work place. "Therefore it hits both honour and pride when they are put ashore and risk losing faith in themselves as fishermen. A fisherman is an individualist and not much used to talking to others about his problems." At a public meeting in Lofoten in January 1990 she presented eight commandments for the preservation of mental health in a crisis period:

• Don't be ashamed.
• Don't isolate yourself.
• Keep the family together.
• Seek out others, agree to meet at the work place if possible.
• Keep up the daily routine.
• Talk about your troubles—others have similar ones.
• Be careful with alcohol.
• Look for help if the worries are getting too bad.

DEMAND TO THE AUTHORITIES

"The fishermen and their families must get immediate catastrophe help," said the fisherwomen on Sørøya in Hasvik municipality, who during the summer of 1989 created a nation-wide action committee supported by the Norwegian Fisherwomen's Association. There were many such demands and from many quarters. Among them were demands that the Fishermen's Bank (Fiskarbanken) and Housing Bank (Husbanken) allow deferred payments and that the scope of the annual government fisheries support be increased.

The authorities responded by raising the support agreement from 900 million Norwegian Kroner in 1989 to 1,125 million in 1990. It was far below what the Norwegian Fishermen's Association had asked for but it was still more than double the amount for 1988, when the total support was 548 million. In particular, price subsidies, unemployment insurance and support to reduce the capacity of the fleet and the fish processing industry were increased.

In addition, in 1990, an extraordinary so-called "coastal package" of 126 million Norwegian Kroner was approved to help with interest and delayed payments on loans to the Housing Bank and the Fishermen's Bank (among others) and as support to the fish processing industry for further readjustment of capacity. Support was also given to factory trawlers so that they could move their activities outside the Norwegian zone, and some have gone as far away as New Zealand. Departments other than the Department of Fisheries also provided crisis help. Funds to retrain the unemployed were approved. A so-called "initiative zone" for North Troms and Finnmark was established, to provide fee and tax exemptions to both private individuals and businesses.

The measures were well received along the coast, even though some felt that it was too little too late; 1990 and 1991 were still tough years. It must be remembered that the fish quotas were lower than ever before. Furthermore, in 1990, the authorities introduced vessel quotas for the whole fleet for the first time in the history of the fisheries. Until then, only the trawlers had been regulated in this way. But the fishermen accepted that strict regulatory measures were necessary and expressed little opposition to the new fisheries regime. In his annual report for 1990, the fisheries counsellor in Skjervøy pointed out that when "the fishermen have managed as well as they have, this only shows how thrifty they are."

How have the fishing industry and the coastal communities in general managed during the crisis? Have doomsday prophecies come true? What about the effect of the crisis measures taken by the authorities? The remainder of this chapter will be devoted to these questions.

REDUCED INCOME

At first glance the official statistics are somewhat surprising. The export value of Norwegian fish products continued to rise in 1989, 1990 and 1991. (See Tables in the Appendix). It would therefore seem that there was no fisheries crisis. These figures, however, include all products, even farmed salmon. The export value of cod in 1990 was 74 percent of the average for the years 1986–1989. This is an indication that the fisheries crisis has had specific regional impact, since the most cod-dependent fishing districts are in North Norway and particularly in Finnmark.

The value of the catch, that is, the value of raw fish going to the fishermen, shows a still greater decline. In Finnmark, the 1990 catch value of cod was reduced to 45 percent of the average value for the years 1986 to 1989. For Troms and Nordland, the figures are 49 and 77 percent, respectively. When we look at fish species as a whole (not including farmed salmon), then the picture is somewhat better. For Finnmark, the total value of the catch for 1990 was 62 percent, for Troms 82 and for Nordland 92 percent.

In the three northernmost provinces, only the fishermen in Nordland managed to shift their efforts to fishing for species other than cod. The size of the catch of other fish species increased by a good 7 percent from 1989 to 1990. In the rest of North Norway, the supply of other fish species declined; in Finnmark the decrease was 21 percent and in Troms 40 percent. Many of the other fish species, such as haddock and pollock, were also in poor supply and therefore subjected to strict quota regulations.

When the export value does not show a reduction even though the value of the catch does, this indicates that the catch sector was hit harder than the processing and export sectors. The main reason is that the fish processing industry can get supplies from abroad, primarily from Russia. If such supplies were included, then the 1990 catch value for Finnmark would be only 75 percent of what it was before the crisis (all fish species), while the figure for Troms would be 84 percent. In 1991, the landing of Russian raw material influenced the statistics so much that the catch value was above the average value for the period 1986–1989.

Nevertheless, the reduction in catch value was less than the reduction in the amount caught. Thus, while the total catch value for Finnmark in 1990 was 62 percent of the average for the years 1986 to 1989, the total amount caught was at 40 percent, and in 1991 it was 68 and 69 percent, respectively. In Troms, the catch value for 1990 was 82 percent of the average value for the three years prior to the crisis, while the amount caught was 55 percent. For Nordland, the figures were 86 percent and 76 percent, respectively. In other words, the price increase helped to compensate for the reduced fish quotas which the crisis had brought with it. This is not only the market mechanism at work; the fishermen also work to make sure they deliver the best possible quality fish to fetch the highest possible prices. Reports during 1990 indicated that the fishermen were cautious about going out in bad weather, and so missed hauling their nets on time, thereby reducing the quality of the fish.

South Norway hardly noticed the fisheries crisis, at least when considering the value of the fish landed. In 1990, the value was 99 percent of the average for the years 1986 to 1989. However, South Norwegian fishermen are quite active in North Norway and land some of their northern catches there. As a consequence, they are partially subject to the strict quota regulations in the north.

HIGH AND DRY

Even though a price increase has offset some of the effects of these low quotas, the reduction in income has nevertheless been significant. The fishermen have every reason to despair. It is difficult to predict accurately what long-term consequences the crisis will have. The short-term effects, however, can be seen from official statistics.

Statistics confirm that the fear of losing house and boat is realistic; figures from the State Fishermen's Bank (Statens Fiskarbank) show that in 1989 and 1990 there were almost triple the usual number of bankruptcy auctions. Most of the bankruptcies were in North Norway, but the proportional increase was greatest in South Norway. Processing firms, as well as vessels, went bankrupt.

In 1991, after the authorities had introduced the extraordinary support measures, the trend changed. While the number of vessel bankruptcies in North Norway in 1990 (including North Trøndelag) was 295 percent of the average for the years 1985–1987, in 1991 it was down to 141 percent. The figures also show that the avalanche of bankruptcies started as early as 1988, that is, two years before the big crisis year.

To lose one's boat is serious, but it is an even greater tragedy when one has to leave house and home. Then one is indeed left high and dry. The Housing Bank can present some bleak figures. (Like the Fishermen's Bank, this is a state-owned bank; it was established to create reasonably-priced housing for ordinary people.) In North Troms and Finnmark, the number of distraint auctions for 1990 was almost double (191 percent) the average for the years 1986 to 1989. In the fisheries municipalities in the remainder of North Norway, the increase was 42 percent. However, even here, it appears that the government's support measures have been effective. In 1991, the number of auctions decreased considerably (136 percent in North Troms and Finnmark, 94 percent in the remainder of the North Norwegian fishing municipalities in relation to the average for 1986–89).

UNEMPLOYMENT

It doesn't take long to fill the fish quotas and so many fishermen are soon at home sitting idle. The next phase is a reduced economy ashore. The fish processing plants start laying people off; there are fewer boat repairs, and the fishermen no longer demand products and services to the same degree as previously. In brief, there is a severe impact on the labour market in fishing communities.

However, the statistics show that the fishing municipalities had a considerably greater unemployment rate than the national average even before the crisis hit. The national unemployment rate as a whole was 3.9 percent for the years 1986 to 1989 while, for the fishing municipalities, it was 6 percent. Finnmark was, as expected, in the worst situation. There the average figure for fishing municipalities was 8.8 percent.

In 1990 the situation became significantly worse. For the country as a whole, the figure rose to 11 percent, the highest recorded unemployment since the 1930s.[2] Unemployment created concern in political quarters and among the authorities. For the fishing municipalities the situation was far more serious. In 1990, the average unemployment rate there was 12.3 percent. Again, Finnmark was hardest hit, with an unemployment rate in the fishing municipalities as high as 22.9 percent. For fishing municipalities in Troms and Nordland, the unemployment rate was 11.5 and 13 percent, respectively. In 1990 the average figures for all types of municipalities were 9.6 percent for Nordland, Troms 10.4 percent and Finnmark 15.3 percent. In other words, the fishing municipalities received the hardest blows.

There were considerable variations between fishing municipalities. Worst off were the three Finnmark municipalities, Måsøy, Lebesby and Loppa (see map 4). The first had an increase from an average of barely 6 percent for the years 1986 to 1989, to 32.6 percent in 1990. Table 1 shows "the top ten" fishing municipalities with the highest unemployment.

Table 1 Fishing municipalities with the greatest unemployment,* 1990

	Unemployment 1990 %	Average Unemployment 1986-1988 %
Måsøy	32.6	5.9
Lebesby	24.1	8.5
Loppa	22.2	3.6
Osen	22.1	8.9
Bø	22.0	9.9
Øygarden	21.9	9.4
Flakstad	21.2	8.1
Hasvik	19.0	7.3
Værøy	18.3	7.7
Kvalsund	16.5	8.5

Source: Norwegian Social Science Data Services (Norsk samfunnsvitenskapelig datatjeneste).
* Unemployment as a percentage of registered workers.

FEWER FISHERMEN?

It is likely that the fishing crisis will contribute to the post-war trend of fewer and fewer fishermen. A look at the Fishermen's Census will confirm this. The decrease from 1989 to 1991 more than doubled when compared to the decrease during the three-year period prior to the crisis. For the country as a whole, the decrease in the number of fishermen from 1986 to 1989 was 567 persons, while the drop from 1989 to 1991, was 1,445 persons. The pattern is the same for both parts of the country and for the three North Norwegian provinces.

As expected, North Norway showed the greatest decrease. In comparison to 1988, the decrease was 12.8 percent, while South Norway experienced a drop of 5.7 percent. The number of full-time fishermen is then somewhat evenly distributed over the two parts of the country (North Norway—11,157, South Norway—10,891). Of the North Norwegian provinces, Finnmark experienced the greatest decline—13.5 percent.

The table below shows the ten municipalities with the greatest decrease in the number of fishermen. Utsira, a small fishing community on Vestlandet, tops the list with a dramatic drop of more than 30 percent from 1988 to 1991. Less dramatic, but nevertheless significant, is the reduction in Lebesby in Finnmark. Osen and Roan, two municipalities in the province of Trøndelag, are also among the top ten. Thus, even though it is evident that the North Norwegian municipalities are experiencing the greatest drop in the number of fishermen, individual municipalities and communities in South Norway are also hard hit.

Table 2   Fishing municipalities with the greatest reduction in the number of full-time fishermen

	Reduction in no. of fishermen, 1988-1991 %
Utsira	34.4
Lebesby	19.4
Loppa	18.3
Mindsund	22.0
Ibestad	17.7
Roan	15.5
Karlsøy	14.9
Osen	14.3
Bjarkøy	14.3
Berg	13.7

Source: The Fishermen's Census (Fiskeridirektoratet).

NEW OUTMIGRATION WAVE?

In post-war Norway the pattern has been that the coastal municipalities have been drained by people moving to towns or densely
populated areas in search of work. This would lead one to think that
such an increase in unemployment as we have witnessed here would
result in increased movement out of the fishing municipalities.
However, the figures show the opposite. A total of 40 of the country's
439 municipalities are classified as fishing municipalities by the
Central Bureau of Statistics. More than half (21) of these have
actually experienced a reduction in the numbers of people leaving
since the full impact of the fisheries crisis was felt. The fishing
municipalities in North Norway have generally experienced less net
outmigration (outmigration minus inmigration) since 1989 than in
the previous three-year period. In the fishing municipalities in
Finnmark the net outmigration in 1990 was reduced by 15 percent
compared to the three-year period from 1986 to and including 1988,
and the rate of outmigration was still decreasing in 1991. An even
greater decrease occurred in Troms and Nordland, where, the net
outmigration has been halved. Outmigration has been far more
unfavourable to the South Norwegian fishing municipalities, which
have seen an actual quadrupling by comparison with the period
1986–88. But then, the fishing municipalities in the South have
usually been far better off in terms of outmigration than the municipalities in the North.

As with the unemployment, there are also differences between
fishing municipalities in population trends. During the crisis period,
many municipalities found that more people were leaving than
coming. The "top ten" list is presented below.

Table 3 Fishing municipalities with the greatest decline in population 1989-1991

	Net outmigration 1989-1991 as percent of 1988 population %	Increase in average net outmigration between years 1986-1988 and 1989-1991 %
Lebesby	6.5	161
Røst	6.0	56
Torsken	5.5	104
Værøy	5.4	87
Bjarkøy	5.0	131
Øksnes	4.7	125
Loppa	4.6	38
Bø	4.6	127
Karlsøy	4.6	78
Træna	4.5	3.50

Source: Norwegian Social Science Data Services (Norsk samfunnsvitenskapelig
datajeneste).

All municipalities on the top ten list are North Norwegian. Lebesby, in East Finnmark, is the fishing municipality in the country which has had the greatest net outmigration since the fishing crisis started. Here, there has also been a considerable deterioration in relation to previous times; it is second from the top on the list of fishing municipalities with the highest unemployment rate in 1990. Four of the municipalities on the top ten list, however, show a considerable improvement. On Røst in Nordland, and Loppa in Finnmark, the decrease in net outmigration has been noticeably large. As far as Røst is concerned, it might be that we are seeing the effects of the optimism created through the "coastal action" headed by the mayor. If so, then the other municipalities could learn from Røst, even though, admittedly, Røst was not as hard hit by quota reductions as the fishing municipalities farther north.[3]

The main pattern, therefore, has been that the move away from the fishing municipalities slowed, rather than accelerated, after the fishing crisis hit. The explanation for this unexpected phenomenon can only be the generally high unemployment in the country. There are no longer many other places one can go and find a job. It is nevertheless interesting to determine that the fishing crisis has not contributed to the depopulation of the coast. People would rather be unemployed where they are, as long as they at least have a place to live.

RESCUE IN SIGHT?

In summary, the figures show that the fisheries crisis is real enough, even though the total export value has not declined. But the crisis has been found to be more regional than national. It is North Norway, particularly the northernmost province of Finnmark, which has been hardest hit, though the trend is disquieting for the South Norwegian fishing municipalities as well. Many families have worked very hard yet lost both income and property.

Some factors do, however, help to mitigate the effects of the crisis. The low quotas have been forcing up the price to the fishermen and therefore the loss of income has been smaller than it might have been. Support measures by the authorities have helped to ease the situation somewhat. So have the Russian supplies of raw material which the authorities are encouraging by amending the Sea Limit Act ('Sjøgrenseloven').[4] Previously, foreign vessels were prohibited from landing fish in Norwegian ports without a special permit from the Norwegian authorities. The Act was amended so that now foreign landings are legal unless the authorities decide otherwise.

Last but not least, in 1991 there were reasons to increase the quotas. The fishermen had observed large populations of cod along the coast and pressured the authorities to ease the restrictions. In consultation with researchers, the authorities reacted by increasing the cod quota from 113,000 tonnes in 1990 to 128,500 tonnes in 1991. This was not much, but it was a step in the right direction. However, the fishermen felt strongly that the vessel quota system was not fair, and wanted changes, particularly for the smallest vessels. These have now come under a competitive system which has a total allowable catch for the fleet. In 1991, an intense debate developed concerning transferable quotas, with the authorities in favour and the fishermen against.

The collective depression which characterized the industry during the fall of 1989 and through 1990 is slowly giving way; people are beginning to feel that there may, perhaps, be rescue in sight. Just as the dark period ends in January in North Norway and the sun starts to get higher in the sky, life has suddenly become easier to live, even though it is still dark outside for most of the day.

Why Everything Goes Wrong   3

The American biologist Garret Hardin was the first to use the expression "the tragedy of the commons," writing about overpopulation in *Science* in 1968. He used the following as an illustration of this concept: Imagine a common pasture. Every shepherd will try to graze as many animals as possible on the pasture. He will ask himself, what will be my return if I increase my herd by one more animal? The calculation for the individual, says Hardin, has a positive and a negative side. The positive side consists of increased income in the form of milk and meat. The negative is the extra load on the pasture which the new animal represents. But since the negative effect is distributed among all those who have animals there, the added cost to the individual will be negligible; the calculation for each shepherd shows a surplus. Therefore, they will continue to bring more and more animals to the pasture until catastrophe overtakes them, that is, the pasture is ravaged.

In other words, the tragedy is an unavoidable result of each shepherd acting in a manner which, for him, is rational. Garret Hardin is often quoted as follows:

> Each man is locked into a system that compels him to increase his herd without limit—in a world that is limited. Ruin is the destination toward which all men rush, each pursuing his own interest in a society that believes in the freedom of the commons. Freedom in a commons brings ruin to all.

EVERYBODY'S PROPERTY—NOBODY'S PROPERTY

Many people are of the opinion that the fisheries crisis is an expression of the "tragedy of the commons." To look at the problem this way indicates that the problems go deep, because the crisis is caused by the resource itself—the fact that the fish is free to all.

Nobody owns the fish which swim in the ocean. Everybody can fish wherever and whenever they wish. There are no limits on how much one can catch, except the fish themselves and the costs involved in catching them. This is the key problem of the commons. As the Canadian economist, Scott Gordon (1954), pointed out, "Everybody's property is nobody's property." And what nobody owns, nobody is responsible for managing.

Under such circumstances the fisherman has little reason to show moderation. He cannot expect to profit by limiting his catch while waiting for the fish to grow larger, because when the time comes to harvest the increment it would already have been caught by others. So there is no point in waiting; rather, it is important to go after it, and the sooner the better.

From the point of view of the individual fisherman, this is rational if short-sighted behaviour. But common sense disappears if we broaden the perspective to the whole group of fishermen. Individual and collective interests are then headed for a collision.

PROFITABILITY

Nature's abundance could, if utilized properly, provide a profit beyond the normal return on investment.[1] Normal return here means what the fisherman may earn by using his labour and capital in alternate activity. This added profit is called resource rent. From a socio-economic point of view, it would be proper to ensure that it remains as large as possible.

As long as the fish provide resource rent, the individual fisherman will gain by increasing his investment. With no restrictions on the catch, market equilibrium will occur when all fishermen reach the point of normal profit. But then the fisheries will provide no resource rent.

When, on the other hand, maximum rent is desired, the following must occur: The total yield must be limited, so as to ensure the fish stock's ability to renew itself. However, that alone is not enough. If a total quota only is established, the cost-driven competition to catch the biggest share will only be heightened. There must also be restrictions on what is employed to catch the fish: investment, amount of equipment and participation. The number of new fishermen must also be reduced; the fisheries must become a closed shop. This is where the government gets into the act. To protect the fishermen against themselves, the authorities must put regulatory measures into effect. If the tragedy has not already happened in all fisheries, then, according to theory, it is only a matter of time before it does—unless the authorities step in.

TRIAL AND ERROR

That, briefly, is the commons theory as it applies in the fishing industry. Authorities, both in Norway and many other countries, have found theoretical reasons for implementing strict regulations. Regulation of the fisheries, however, has been a process characterized by trial and error both nationally and internationally. It has often had unfortunate side effects, and sometimes the results have been diametrically opposite to those intended. When the authorities established limits on the length of boats, the fishermen simply made them wider; this affected their seaworthiness and energy consumption. When the fishing season was shortened, they simply increased the amount of equipment; this led to poorer quality fish. When quotas were introduced, only the biggest and most valuable fish were caught, while the rest were dumped over the side. As a result of such manoeuvres, oceanographers have trouble getting an overview of the quantities of stocks caught.

When looking at it in this way, we may ask ourselves whether the crisis on the coast today is caused in spite of, or because of, the regulations enforced by the authorities. The answer is likely to be both. The problems the authorities wanted to correct have only been compounded by the regulatory measures now employed.

With the exception of geographically limited fisheries (such as the Lofoten fisheries), the regulation of fisheries is a relatively new phenomenon in Norway. It is particularly since the introduction of the licensing arrangements at the beginning of the 1970s that we can talk about a regulated fishery. The licensing system has, however, produced dubious results, both in Norway and in other fishing nations. It has not helped prevent the build-up of over-capacity nor the concentration in certain geographic areas. In Norway, the view is that it has fostered a "licensing aristocracy"—a fishery for the privileged.

The introduction of the 200-nautical-mile economic zone has also had many negative consequences internationally. It signalled that now resource problems would be solved once and for all. The warning of its introduction alone created optimism in many countries and contributed to the enormous new investment with its subsequent far too great catching capacity.

MURPHY'S LAW

The tragedy of the commons is a major challenge for those who must regulate. Even if the authorities were able to limit new effort, the fishermen's interest in increasing their share of the catch would not be diminished. It is profitable for the individual fisherman to breach or circumvent the regulations if he is not likely to get caught doing so. As with the shepherd, the added income from overexploitation goes to the one who does it. The negative effect on the stock is distributed among everybody.

Nothing is better for the poacher than for the government to control everybody else. The fishermen may pay lip service to government attempts to regulate but, in practice, the temptation to look for a loophole is too great. The fisheries crisis has uncovered serious breaches of the regulations. It is not for nothing that the Canadian fisheries economist Parzival Copes (1986) concludes that the fisheries regulations are subject to Murphy's Law: "Whatever can go wrong will go wrong."

Regulations are meant to prevent tragedy, but they entail "tragic" choices. To close the fisheries to newcomers trying to make a living poses a moral problem comparable to the life-boat dilemma—what's to be done when the lifeboat is full? Should one more be taken aboard at the risk of sinking, or should those aboard row hard to get away from all those crying to be saved? Downsizing the fleet to create a better relationship between the resource and catching capacity is regarded by the authorities as the main task in the next few years. However, downsizing the capacity will affect the fisheries communities, which are vulnerable and likely to collapse because the fishermen are not only competitors but also dependent on each other in significant areas.

Regulations not only intrude into the fishery, but they also affect vibrant local communities which must function if fishing is to be continued, and if they are to be attractive places to live. "A lifeboat which does not function to a certain extent as a community will not manage to bring its human cargo ashore," says the American economist Kenneth Boulding (1977).

TRANSFERABLE QUOTAS

If regulations are necessary due to the advanced technology available to modern fishermen, the method of regulating is still in dispute. The fisheries economists are in favour of dividing up and privatizing the commons. Individual transferable quotas (ITQs), whereby fishermen can buy and sell their quotas, are the present tune. The argument is that this will promote greater flexibility and efficiency in the fisheries. New Zealand and Iceland are held up as models of this arrangement.

Twenty years of experience with fishing regulations should have taught us that there is no single way to solve all the problems. Side effects always appear after a while. Reports from New Zealand and Iceland indicate that a complete solution has not yet been found; there is still dumping of small fish and regional concentration, and those with the most capital win.

Individual transferable quotas entail a radical transformation of the regulatory system by having the market mechanism take over. The results of this are unpredictable. As Østerud (1979) maintained, the market, when given free rein, has a tendency to follow the path of least resistance. It is thus rather uncertain how the coastal culture will come out of this. In addition, once the system has been introduced, it is difficult to turn back if that should become necessary. It is much simpler to grant rights than to take them back. It might therefore be advisable to wait and learn from what is happening in other countries before we take similar steps. It appears, though, that the Norwegian authorities are impatient. Just before the summer of 1991, the Department of Fisheries presented a paper which suggested transferable quotas be introduced. The recommendations are controversial within the industry.

REGIONALIZATION

Another solution which has been put forward by, among others, the Regional Committee for North Norway and Namdalen,[2] is to distribute the Norwegian quota between regions. The expectation is that this will improve on the regionally uneven distribution of catches which over the years has resulted in the North Norwegian provinces and Finnmark, in particular, coming out the losers. In recent years, more and more of the raw material caught off the coast of Finnmark has been brought south, and the province's own fleet has lost much of its share of the profits.

Regionalization would mean pursuing the principle behind the rationale for establishing the 200-nautical-mile economic zone on a smaller geographical scale, that is, giving the provinces or national regions greater control over the management of the fisheries resources. This has been done in the U.S.A. The three coasts are divided into a total of eight regions with their own regulatory councils whose task is to develop regulations for their regions. In cases where stocks move between the regions, the councils negotiate how to distribute the resources. The law does not permit discrimination between fishermen based on where they come from. The success of the system so far is attributed to the setting of borders between the regions to correspond as closely as possible to the ecosystem. This cuts down on the amount of negotiation.

Perhaps this regulatory system could not only ensure economic sustainability in the Norwegian fishing industry as a whole, but could also benefit a province like Finnmark. It is not difficult to see problems with such an arrangement. What about the great mobility among Norwegian fishermen? Seasonal fisheries, such as the Lofoten and Finnmark fisheries, have always drawn fishermen from far away. Regionalization cannot block the migratory pattern of the fish, only that of the fishermen. The U.S.A. example nevertheless shows that this problem can be addressed.

FAIRNESS

The key problem appears to be to get the fishermen to place their common interests ahead of their personal interests. What does it take to get the individual fisherman to identify with the regulations so strongly that he will voluntarily adhere to them, even though in the short term he will lose thereby? Fishermen's reaction to regulations at present suggests that they value fairness above all.

Regulations which are contrary to the fishermen's sense of fairness will not have much chance of success. If there is a sense of injustice, one feels less bound by the regulations. It is rather difficult to determine what is fair. It is not necessarily fair to treat everyone equally. For example, equal quotas for all would favour the older paid-up vessels, while the new modern boats with high capital cost would get the short end of the stick. Therefore, special treatment is sometimes necessary in order to ensure fair treatment.

Another problem is acquiring enough local knowledge to ensure fairness. Periods when fishing is banned are fine for some fishermen and bad for others, depending on when they have their best seasons. There are also variations between districts, equipment groups and boat sizes. Experience gained from 1990 shows that many pensioners got quotas, whereas young, newly-established fishermen were left out. In Finnmark, the fjord fishermen, many of whom are coastal Saami, have been hurt. They combine fishing with other activities and often cannot show the necessary quantity from the previous year to qualify for a quota. To be sure, fishing provides only a portion of their income, but it is nevertheless crucial in balancing the family budget.

Throughout history, fishermen have been concerned with securing regulations which all can live with. For that reason, the Lofoten fishery has always been open and regulations to the contrary have met with protest actions. However, the Lofoten fishery is open in a special way. Anyone can participate in the Lofoten Sea, but not with all types of gear everywhere. In this respect, the Lofoten fishery is regulated in greater detail than any other fishery.

RIGHTS

Some solutions to the tragedy of the commons go not only against the people's sense of fairness, but against their perception of the law. Whether the fishermen have time-honoured rights to their area, or the fish that swim there, is a legal question not yet resolved. This problem has been raised in particular relation to the Saami population. Norwegian Saami National Association (Norske Samers Riksforbund) has maintained that the Saami, as a group, have the same rights to marine resources as they have to land and water. This view has been supported by the legal community, and the Department of Fisheries appears to accept it. But some have argued that the entire population of Northern Norway should have corresponding rights.

It may appear paradoxical that in the U.S.A., unlike Norway, legislation has emphasized the importance of local culture in regulating the fisheries, since proponents of the market mechanism have traditionally been on firmer ground there than here. Norway does recognize cultural components to a degree. The core of the Magnussen Act is "Optimum Yield," a broader concept than "Maximum Sustainable Yield" or "Maximum Economic Yield," both of which are well-known in the professional literature on the fisheries. "Optimum yield" places the emphasis precisely on considerations of cultural and social aspects of the fishery.[3]

The American concern for cultural rights in fisheries regulatory policy is probably due to the fisheries being carried out, to a great extent, by certain ethnic groups (Indians, Vietnamese, Portuguese, Norwegians, for example) in local communities where one group dominates. The cultural variations are visible to both the minority and majority population.

SELF-REGULATION

It has been maintained that the tragedy of the commons is a misleading term because it mixes two things which should be kept separate, that is, common property and free access. The traditional Norwegian commons institution was definitely not a system which guaranteed free access for everyone and in which behaviour was unrestricted. The commons was often a common pasture controlled by a village association and jointly managed by its members.

There are no Norwegian studies showing the existence of such local commons systems at sea, as they exist in many other countries. However, sufficient research has been carried out to determine that the fishermen often cooperate closely on the fishing grounds. They do not work strictly alone and in competition with each other as is assumed by the commons theory. There is often informal cooperation to avoid collisions, as when the fishermen coordinate the setting and hauling of nets. It is also common practice to respect each others' time-honoured right to set gear in specific locations.

In Lofoten, this cooperation is formalized by separate regulations and organized through a committee arrangement by which the fishermen themselves set down the regulations. The committees control the use of gear and area distribution, but not the total catch or distribution of quotas. A basis for conflict nevertheless exists. To distribute areas among various equipment groups, where fishermen have opposing interests, is a conflict-charged matter. But at the same time, they have a common interest in reaching an agreement or there would be chaos out on the grounds. They have managed to create this type of agreement, even though the differences in the Lofoten Sea have been many and harsh at times. Not least, they have maintained the agreement by retaining a regulatory system in which the fishermen have had influence and control for almost 100 years (Jentoft and Kristoffersen 1989). From a commons theoretical point of view, this is extraordinary.

PRACTICAL POLICY

The fact that regulatory arrangements initiated by fishermen actually exist has caused some researchers to refute the commons theory and its premises. They maintain that the theory is not representative of the actual conditions in the fisheries. The competition between fishermen and their supposed individualism does not override all other behaviours. The fishermen cooperate when they are served by doing so. The commons does not stop fishermen from following rules and norms.

The commons theory does not allow for structural differences in the fishing industry, but treats all fishermen equally. In logical reasoning, where the aim is to deduce certain consequences from given conditions, this is fine. A problem arises, however, when a theory is taken as the basis for a practical policy, if one neglects to check whether it agrees with actual conditions. Reality is then replaced by the model and there is a risk of doing more harm than good.

A problem with Garret Hardin's theory is that it is so seductive. It is logical and simple, and if you understand the reasoning then you think you understand the world. No attempt is made to look at how reality functions. Competition, individualism and the fact that the fishermen have the same goals are taken for granted, but what is forgotten is that the fishermen can also cooperate and stand together if the structural prerequisites are present. The opportunities available through cooperative solutions to regulatory problems, such as in the Lofoten fisheries, are then overlooked. Instead, the answer tends to be detailed government control and thorough inspection methods. The result could easily become the opposite of what was envisaged. The fishermen oppose the regulations rather than follow them. I will return to this problem in a later chapter.

The Fish Processing Industry in a Bind 4

Like the fishermen, the plants on shore are dependent on a regulatory system which actually functions. The resource crisis has therefore landed the fish processing industry in difficulty. As well, the fish processing industry must adapt to unpredictable export markets. It has to tackle uncertainties on two fronts.

While the raw material situation appears bleak, marketing prospects appear more promising. Fish has become a popular food, not least for health reasons. Research has developed new technologies and new types of products from fish raw material which show promise for the future. At the same time, fish farming has become a new and important addition to many plants. Not only have new niches been opened up in the market, but more stable servicing of the market is apparent.

NEW OPORTUNITIES

Technological research has introduced a new dynamic element into the fish processing industry. Research has progressed of its own momentum, outside and independent of individual plants. Many of the plants appear to be unable to utilize research results because they lack the necessary expertise. For that reason, there is a risk that innovations occurring within, for example, biotechnological research, will bypass the established fish processing firms.

New opportunities in production technology and marketing clearly reveal a gap in expertise which must be filled. It is encouraging that the Coastal Expertise Committee (1990) is promoting an action plan for management development in the fish processing industry, but more than a single effort is needed. The firms cannot hope to fill the expertise gap once and for all. They will always be faced with the need to upgrade their expertise. This is not unique to the fish processing industry; many industries have to meet similar challenges.

How do such challenges affect the fish processing industry? How realistic is it to assume that the firms will manage to meet them? What is needed to achieve this?

BUSINESS CULTURE

Expertise is partly the result of practical experience and partly the result of education. It is characteristic of leaders in the fish processing industry that they are long on trade experience but short on education. Long experience may compensate somewhat for a lack of education. On the other hand, many years of education cannot replace experience. Much of the knowledge needed to manage a fish processing plant must be learned on the job. The ideal manager is, of course, one who has a combination of both.

A study of organizational and managerial conditions in the fish processing industry in North Norway, carried out by the author for the Coastal Expertise Committee and cited throughout this chapter, found that six out of ten plant managers had no education beyond Grade 7 (Jentoft 1990). Many had taken courses, but most of these had been of short duration. Only eight percent had more than one year of financial/administrative education, while only two percent had education of comparable length in production technology.

The study also found little turnover in management. About 40 percent of top managers had at least twenty years in that position. It was found that recruitment of managers occurs mostly within their own business and rarely outside the trade. Less than two percent had come from positions outside the fishing industry, while a good 18 percent had been recruited from other fish processing plants. There is clearly an inside market for managers, where trade experience is the main factor.

In many ways, it is important to emphasize experience. But such large internal recruitment results in plants missing out on the learning and stimulus inherent in recruiting managers from completely different professions and environments. This could mean that the fish processing industry is being "fenced in." Particular problem-solving techniques and standards for good management and effective organization are developed. To put it simply, a special culture is created in the fish processing industry. Such a culture may function in response to changes and opportunities for development originating within the branch of industry itself, but at the same time, it may make the branch less open to external challenges from, for example, various research environments.

The internal recruitment of managers may be related to the fact that as many as half of the enterprises are family businesses, where a change in management is linked to generational change. However, the same study found that internal recruitment for top management positions is at least as high in fish processing enterprises with other types of ownership structures.

BUSINESS STRUCTURE

As a rule, the fish processing industry consists of small and medium-sized firms. Three out of four have fewer than fifty employees, while one out of three has less than ten. Compared with competing countries, such as Canada, Iceland and the Faeroe Islands, our firms are, on the average, smaller (see Apostle and Jentoft 1991; Dalsà 1987).

Norway's fish processing industry consists of many small units because fishing is carried out all along the coast by small vessels from small communities. Part of the explanation can also be found in the manner in which the fishing industry is organized.

The industry is characterized by relatively little vertical integration. It is exceptional for a firm to include the whole production chain from catch through processing to export. Fishing is mainly carried out by independent fishermen, while marketing and export is carried out by independent exporters or sales organizations. Our study found that 35 percent of the firms have owner-interest in vessels, one-third carry out direct export, while 15 percent are involved in both sides.

This "layered" organizational structure is, to a great degree, politically controlled through legislation which has prevented the firms from expanding vertically. The regulations concerning rights of ownership of fishing vessels have ensured the fishermen control over catching, while the Export Act has given the export link dominance over marketing and sales. This is particularly the case for dried and salt fish. The export of frozen fish is carried out by organizations such as FRIONOR and Nordic Group, which includes members of the fish processing industry (Hallenstvedt 1982).

Indeed, we could say that the settlement pattern has made a small-scale fish processing industry inevitable, legislation has made it unavoidable, and organization has made it possible. The fact that the plants have left the demanding tasks of marketing and export to others has made it possible to operate with a smaller organization than would otherwise be necessary. Also, the plants have not been forced into building up expertise in marketing and export.

The layered form of organization has been seen as a rational solution to a structural problem. There are efficiency gains to be realized in transferring marketing and export to export agencies with special expertise. However, this form of organization also has problems. It weakens the learning environment at the plant level. Indirect market contact provides the plants with only second-hand knowledge of market developments. Not only are the managers deficient in marketing education, but they don't get a chance to learn by experience. This is a problem which has lately been subject to closer scrutiny by, among others, The Coastal Expertise Committee. Recognition of the problem has contributed to amendment of the Export Act so as to allow integration further on the chain.

MARKET ORIENTATION

The crisis in Norway teaches us that the growth and developmental possibilities of the fish processing industry must be encouraged primarily in relation to the market. New markets must be found for new products, and quality products must be made available. Fish is food, and people are fussy about what they eat, particularly if they have to pay a high price for the product.

There are many interesting dimensions in this regard. Until now, the expansion of the fish processing industry has been based on the supply of raw material. Plants have expanded by increasing the amount of raw material, often at the expense of other plants. With a limited resource base, growth for one can only mean loss for the other. Growth based on the market, however, does not mean the same zero sum game. In relation to the market, firms need not be fewer to be bigger. In a regional perspective this is important: growth does not need to be a threat to small communities.

Poor quality fish cannot be restored further along in the production chain. If poor quality is brought into the processing hall, little can be done to upgrade the quality at the filleting table. This places strict demands on quality control in all phases of the production process. Because quality control presumes that the standards of products and all links in the production process are clear to all employees at all times, problems with quality can only be overcome through training and creating a positive attitude in the plant.

ORGANIZATIONAL LEVEL

It is important to clarify the level to which marketing tasks should be assigned. Should they be the domain of organizations on a national level—which has been the case up to now—or should they be linked to regional institutions or should individual plants carry out these tasks?

The disadvantage of a centrally controlled marketing system is, as mentioned before, that it shields the plants from market contacts. It engenders a certain passivity and inhibits more market-oriented management. Our study found that product development does not employ many managers. Only about 20 percent work daily with product development.[1]

On the other hand, it is resource-intensive to decentralize marketing. For example, it is no simple task for small fish processing plants to operate professionally in the American or Japanese markets.

The solution can probably be found somewhere between the two extremes in the form of regional organization. It is dangerous, however, to have too firm an opinion on what organizational model is preferable. The goal must be to achieve both efficiency and market contact at the same time. Joint organization need not result in the firms being deficient in market orientation. It depends on, among other things, the internal organization—how internal communication occurs between levels in the organization.

BARRIERS TO GROWTH

What will happen to individual plants now that the changes in the Fish Export Act make it possible for plants to take over marketing as well as product development?[2] What will be required of management? What organizational consequences will this have? The organizational theory of small firms may provide some indications.

Several researchers have pointed out that in the course of the growth of firms there are built-in barriers which prevent them from growing and developing further (see for example Steinmetz 1969). As a firm grows, it will eventually reach a point where further growth will have organizational consequences. The manager will have to change from direct to indirect management and more formal arrangements for direction and control will be required. The manager must spend more time behind the desk and delegate tasks to others. The administration will have to expand, new expertise must be acquired and the manager and work force must be retrained.

Our study found that it is not primarily the amount of raw material processed by the plant which determines how complex the organization of the plant is. Of more importance is how the raw material is utilized, for example, the degree of further processing. This is also important if the plant carries out export and marketing on its own. Such plants have larger administrations and more employees at the management level than plants which are not themselves involved in exporting. This indicates that plants which grow in relation to the market will meet growth barriers at an earlier stage than those which only grow in volume of raw material.

Clearly, this concerns not only technological and financial barriers, but barriers of a psychological nature and problems of expertise. Rather than leaping over these hurdles, the manager tries to stay below them. He strives to keep the business from growing. Businesses which start out small therefore often remain small.

For an individual plant, this may be a sensible choice. There are many examples of too rapid expansion resulting in catastrophe. However, this attitude also means that opportunities to develop may be lost—opportunities which, had they been seized, could have made an important contribution to the plant and to employment.

PAPERLESS MANAGEMENT

Research in many countries has found that small and medium-sized firms are very dynamic and inventive and that they create many new jobs, both through the creation of new firms and through growth. Small firms have the ability to change rapidly. Large firms are like supertankers—it is difficult to turn them around. There are many examples of small and medium-sized firms in the fish processing industry exhibiting dynamic behaviour. This has resulted in innovative ideas for raw material, products, marketing and personnel. The ability to change rapidly is also seen in small firms which have a flat organizational structure with a short distance from top to bottom. In the fish processing industry, this is evident from the fact that 73 percent of the managers are alone in the job, while 60 percent have no managers at the middle level, that is, above the line supervisor level. In addition, more than half of the managers responded that they participate daily in the production itself, in other words, they work "on the floor." This provides face-to-face contact between managers and employees.

The flexibility of small plants is also related to their more informal and less bureaucratic management style. Decisions are not taken in meetings by voting after long discussions. Instead, "paperless" management is practised, with no written plans or case presentations. Although this ensures action, it does have drawbacks stemming from a lack of expertise in the use of the tools of business economics. The consequence may be a "closed" and authoritarian management style.

Fifty percent of managers in the fish processing industry said that they do not commit their plans to paper. This applies particularly to plants with ten or fewer employees, in which three out of four managers said they did not use such planning. Nine out of ten managers said that they usually pass information to the employees orally, while five out of ten communicated directly to the workers without going through middlemen.

This informal style of management and the flat organizational structure are two sides of the same coin. At their best, they generate energy among the employees, promote cooperation and equality in the organization, and create a productive work environment through developing common motivation. This is mainly the situation in the plants in the fish processing industry, and in the local communities where these plants are located. To some extent, the effect can be measured by the greater labour peace and the lack of conflict which characterize the relationships between management and employees. In this respect, we are favourably situated in Norway compared to the situation in the fish processing industry in many of our competing countries. It is a condition worth nurturing, because it also facilitates the ability to change. The challenge consists of turning it to an international competitive advantage, as the Japanese have done.

SOCIAL RESPONSIBILITY

Although the plants in the fish processing industry are small, they are often key businesses in their local communities. They provide employment for people in the area and act as anchors for the settlement.

They are also key businesses in another sense of the word. In addition to employing many people locally, they provide a broad range of services to other firms and individual operators. The fishermen are particularly dependent on the plants, where they often have access to fuel, repair services, storage facilities, bait sheds, and food. But they can also suffer from plant actions: the plant may give priority to some boats over others because they are larger and more stable as suppliers, for example, or it may recruit people in competition with the fishing fleet.

The managers of a plant in the fish processing industry thus have considerable social responsibility, both on a day-to-day and on a long-term basis. They have heavier burdens than most managers in other industries, as a result of the geographical location of the plant and its role in the local employment system.

The social responsibility of firms has been the subject of debate internationally, as well as in Norway (see Hallenstvedt 1990). It is not just a matter of firms having a moral obligation to shareholders and to society as a whole, but whether they should maintain certain social functions beyond that of production. Managers who perform a coordinating function in the local fishery, for example by ensuring that supply and recruiting problems do not occur in the fishing fleet, have a responsibility beyond the processing of fish. This also applies to managers who are concerned with full employment in the local community.

In Norwegian fishing communities, social responsibility has traditionally been tied to a paternalistic leadership style. The relationship of the old merchant princes to fishing people attests to that. The relationship between fish buyer and fisherman was varied and personal. The purchase and sale of fish was attached to credit for equipment and investment, storage rent and housing. The fish buyer was the one who set the rules.

This relationship between fisherman and fish buyer still exists in the coastal fisheries of many other nations. In Norway it was abolished when the Raw Fish Act was introduced and the State Fishermen's Bank (Statens Fiskarbank) was established.[3] The exercise of social responsibility has thus changed, but not been lost entirely.

How social responsibility is maintained by the present leadership, and how well it works, is worth an empirical study. There is no doubt that we are dealing with part of the role of being a leader of a fish processing plant. This responsibility must not be regarded as a millstone around the manager's neck; on the contrary, the ability to maintain social responsibility will be an important prerequisite to good management. This is because, even in the future, it will be important to avoid effects outside the plant which could undermine the accommodation to other firms and wage earners locally. A sense of social integration is also necessary to ensure support and encouragement of new measures in the home environment.

LOCAL AND INTERNATIONAL

The fish processing industry from Nord Møre and northward, which constitutes the Raw Fish Association's (Råfisklaget) district, consisted of 384 plants in 1990. That is half of what it was in 1970. The

Norwegian Fish Processing Industry's Association (Fiskeindustriens Landsforening) has calculated that should this development continue, there will be about 275 plants by the turn of the century. The future is therefore worrisome for many plants and local communities. But there is also reason for hope. The overcapacity in the processing industry is not so great as it once was, and fisheries authorities now say that it is important to preserve the plants we have.

Political measures alone, however, cannot shape the business structure in the fish processing industry. It is a question of what will be left when the crisis is over. The largest and most modern plants will not necessarily be the ones to survive. They often have large investments to protect and therefore risk closure before the small and labour-intensive plants.

In the long run, marketing is where the greatest challenges will be found. This requires a shift towards market-oriented management. The manager's dilemma is that he cannot consider just one thing, but must turn his attention in several directions. Fish processing plants are caught in a squeeze between resources and markets, both local and international. This presents a special daily challenge. The manager must be able to use a computer as naturally as he wears rubber boots. But if greater market-orientation leads to reduced interest in the local community and the attendant social responsibility, then the gains could be lost in the shuffle.

Are there any alternatives to the large vertically integrated firms which many now consider the solution to structural problems in the fishing industry? The alternative appears to lie in an organizational form based on networking and cooperation instead of subordination and centralized control, which is the chief feature of vertically integrated firms.

CLASSIC DEFINITION

The concept of "networking" was introduced by the British anthropologist J.A. Barnes (1954) in a study of the fishing station at Bremnes in Sunnhordaland. If Eilert Sundt's study (1867/1972) of the fishing station at Haram was the first social scientific fisheries study in Norway, then Barnes' study was the second. The story goes that the concept occurred to Barnes when he saw the nets hung out to dry; in any case, he describes it as follows:

> Each person is, as it were, in touch with a number of other people, some of whom are directly in touch with each other and some of whom are not. Similarly, each person has a number of friends, and these friends have their own friends, some of any one person's friends know each other, others do not. I find it convenient to talk of a social field of this kind as a *network*. The image I have is of a set of points some of which are joined by lines. The points of the image are people, or sometimes groups, and the lines indicate which people interact with each other.

At Bremnes, Barnes found the economic system strongly interwoven into the kinship system, where the same people took part in a number of activities. Bremnes appeared to be a community where there was considerable order and stability. But is also stood out as a very dynamic community. Barnes found it noteworthy that the place was not ruled by any one person; there was no chief.

VALUABLE RELATIONSHIPS

From Barnes' definition we understand that networking has to do with the way in which managers, or firms as organizations, are linked to other actors. The ties which connect the managers to each other are of a special quality, and are different from the ties which exist in a market or a bureaucracy.

While a network consists of persons who know each other and who feel themselves to be members of a community, the actors in the market are "anybody" to each other. In the market, only products or services are of value, not the relationships between the actors. In the network, on the other hand, the relationship between buyer and seller also has value. Here, it is not only what is offered for sale that is of value, but also who is offering it.

Therefore the transactions will also be different. It is like shopping for a used car. Anyone who buys a used car on the market knows that this is a transaction fraught with great uncertainty. This uncertainty is not only because one often lacks the knowledge to assess the car's quality, but one also lacks knowledge of the used car sales staff. Can they be believed? Can they be trusted? The more professional they appear to be, the more suspicious we become.

People who buy a used car from a friend will experience another type of uncertainty. When a car is bought from a friend, one is fairly certain that it will not collapse the next day. If that should happen, the friendship could collapse too, particularly if one suspects that the friend knew the car was in poor condition. The possibility of losing a friendship makes the seller more open and honest. If he wants to remain a friend, he will mention that the fuel pump may give out very soon.

This is not the whole story, however. When one buys a used car from a friend, one often participates in "paradoxical bargaining." As a buyer, not only is one careful not to force the asking price down, but there is also a chance that one will insist on paying more than the seller is asking! The seller may then exclaim "No way, that's too much!" The paradox is that the buyer tries to raise the price while the seller tries to lower it. The explanation for this "reverse" phenomenon is that even the relationship between buyer and seller has economic value when they are friends. The difference between the network price and the market price can be defined as the price the parties are willing to pay to preserve their friendship.

GOAL OR MEANS?

There are many other comparisons between market and network which could emphasize their special characteristics. Networking, for example, is more stable and lasting. It does not require any active steps to preserve it. That is because it is anchored in friendship, family ties, geographic proximity or a business or professional community. One's fellow students not only remain friends for life but also business or professional connections. In the market, on the other hand, the relationship ceases the moment the transaction has been concluded. Relationships there are entered into with an eye to the transaction, while in a network it is normally the opposite. It is a breach of the ethics of friendship to enter into a friendship with thoughts only of gain or exploitation. Friendship is the goal, not just the means.

Networking could also be compared to a business organization. In a firm, trading is more structured. There are formal rules about how to behave, and accurate records of transactions are kept. At the same time, the organization is characterized by hierarchical control. There is no room for free-wheeling transactions where relative pricing or personal ties of friendship determine if a product, an amount or a person will be transferred from Department A to Department B. A market or a network is not managed as a business is managed. When a product is moved from one department to another, that is strictly a management decision.

This does not necessarily mean that all organizational behaviour is of a formal nature. Many studies show that life in a business, as well as the style of management, do have informal sides. Personal and social ties are developed between employees, both within and between departments and levels. These ties can hold outside the firm; people who work together may become personal friends.

An interesting question is what effect such networks have on a firm's internal life. Is it different when the members have networking contacts? Do such connections promote or hinder productivity? Would there be more solidarity and less conflict in the relationship between management and employees? These questions would be worth studying.

MORAL DIMENSION

Networking, rather than markets and hierarchies, characterizes trading locally within the fishing industry. The study referred to in the previous chapter found that 80 percent of managers in the North Norwegian fish processing industry were born and brought up in the

municipalities in which the plants are located. This dictates that
when managers manage, they do so with known faces that they can
place socially. They do not simply conduct the plants in relation to
a market of faceless people or a bureaucracy of "poker" faces. The
conditions for the development of confidence and trust are therefore
good. Another study of the fish processing industry found that the
relationships between management and employees are less rights-
oriented when management and employees are all local people than
when the work force is imported from outside (Midrè and Solberg
1980). This is in keeping with Barnes' point that a network gives
people a feeling of being among equals and leads to the building of
bridges between conflicting interests.

If this applies to a firm internally, then it should also apply
externally. The mechanisms that lead to the creation of trust inside
organizations should also act as confidence-builders between organizations. Plant managers who know each other personally and
who trust each other can enter more easily into business agreements. Who would dare to sign a contract with someone who might
not be trustworthy?

In personal and business-related networking there are moral as
well as business and legal dimensions. In the market, opportunism
is permitted; for example, one might withhold information to ensure
a contract. But when the business agreement is founded on a
trusting personal relationship, such behaviour would be divisive
and ethically reprehensible.

VERTICAL INTEGRATION

The unfeeling market could create too great a degree of uncertainty,
particularly when there are few partners to choose from. Legislation
and normal rules of good business ethics help somewhat, but are
not enough if the stakes are high. Such institutions could compensate to an extent for the absence of trust, but do not, in themselves,
produce trust. That is done by social relationships. In the absence
of such trusted relationships, vertical and horizontal integration
between firms may be a solution.

According to Mark Granovetter (1985), an American sociologist
who has made a seminal contribution to the theory of networking:

> Other things being equal . . . we should expect pressures toward
> vertical integration in a market where transacting firms lack a
> network of personal relations that connect them or where such a
> network eventuates in conflict, disorder, opportunism and malfea-
> sance. On the other hand, where a stable network of relations

mediates complex transactions and generates standards of behaviour between firms, such pressures should be absent.

Modern fish processing demands a stable supply of raw material. This is due to large investments, methods of production and market demands. Not only is sufficient raw material required, but also raw material at the proper time and of the proper quality. This makes plants vulnerable in relation to an independent harvesting link. Cooperation and synchronization of the activities at sea and on land are needed. Large freezer plants have therefore been integrated into the trawler fleet. The trawlers are, by and large, owned and controlled by firms on land, in contrast to the inshore fleet and the purse seine fleet.

A solution to many of the problems created by the fisheries crisis could thus be to create larger business units encompassing the whole production chain from the fishing grounds to the retail link. Many people think that the current legislation which blocks such integration should be modified. Such modification could, of course, make it more difficult to preserve the scattered settlements which depend on geographically spread out and small-scale fishing and fish processing. But you can't make an omelet without breaking some eggs.

But perhaps the advantages of large vertical, integrated production chains could be realised in less drastic ways. Is it possible to preserve the many small units in the processing and catching links by strengthening the connections between them, not through fusion, but through network building? Is this an alternative to the creation of enormous business concerns?

BRANCH PLANTS

Networks are produced in many contexts as alternatives to hierarchies and are particularly recommended as a strategy for small firms. Through networking, "strategic alliances" are established which provide the basis for "flexible specialization." Network building is also recommended as a strategy for regional industrial development (NordREFO 1987).

Such ideas are not foreign to the fishing industry. The National (Norwegian) Fish Processing Industry's Association envisages a future where the plants form regional cooperatives based on the "hub" principle. Four firms in Senja have taken the initiative and established Senja Seafood. These firms have not relinquished their independence, but try to cooperate for their common good. For instance, they might jointly test new technology before they go to acquisition. "With this cooperation, we can test it in one place instead of making four wrong investments." one of the managers commented in *Nordlys*.

In the wake of the crisis, however, many North Norwegian firms are being taken over by South Norwegians, with the result that the decision-making authority is moved out of the local community. Leading industrial representatives in North Norway are warning against increased "branch planting" of this part of the country's industry. Branch plants are included, and rightly so, in a type of network, but are characterized by subordination and centralization of power.

A network can be built as part of an offensive strategy for regional industrial development, as a preventive measure, or as a defensive measure to counter a new branch or closure. The network can be anchored in a supply contract, a joint venture, or other formal type of cooperation. Formalization in itself is not sufficient however; the cooperation must also be informal. In other words, it is important for the network to have both a functional and an emotional side, that is, the network must not only be useful but also enjoyable. It must be possible to activate it spontaneously when needed, without necessarily presuming that a transaction must take place every time. The ties which bind the participants in the network must resist demands that all accounts must be settled right away. The network must permit delayed returns. It is precisely this delay that is a test and a confirmation among the parties that trust is present.

NEW CREATIONS

The network could serve as a permanent source of information. Consultation could take place before acquisition of new technology or ventures into new products and markets. New ideas are transmitted among members. A network also represents a resource for people planning to establish their own firms.

Lene Foss (1989) at the Norwegian College of Fishery Science (Norges Fiskerihøgskole) is working on a research project in which such hypotheses will be tested. She assumes that in the early stages of a newly-established career it is important to have close and strong connections with others. When starting a business, it is important to have some trusted persons who can be consulted for advice about ideas and plans. Above all, moral support is needed. Such persons are often part of one's circle of close friends or family.

Later, when the final step is being taken, someone is needed who can provide opposition and criticism as well as new information. Family and close friends will often provide positive support in any situation, and are not necessarily helpful in sharpening one's wits. What is needed at this stage is advice from people who are more detached from the project. The problem with close and reliable networks is that they make people think alike. They are characteristic of technical inbreeding. It is a little like when a person passes news on to some friends who are themselves friends—they risk hearing the same news many times over.

The learning effect is greater when one consults people with whom one has a more peripheral relationship and who are members of other networks. This has led Granovetter (1973) to maintain that there is "strength in weak ties." The weak ties serve as a bridge between different networks and thereby to other environments of knowledge.

NETWORK BY DECREE?

By building networks, fish processing plants could compensate for great geographic distances, lack of resources, low expertise and little market power. This, again, could create both stability and dynamism in the business and thereby be a good alternative to a hierarchical business organization.

Networks between firms are not established by governmental decree. They seldom come about through regional policies or through other political initiatives. When they are formed, it is because managers themselves are getting involved. It is in the nature of things that networking occurs voluntarily—the parties must want it. Trust is a central ingredient in any network, but cannot be declared at the beginning; it must be built over time and among those who form the network.

Network building, nevertheless, could be recommended as a strategy for governmental action. Instead of working with firms individually, effort could be directed towards groups of firms. Rather than supporting firms individually, support could be given to strengthening contacts between firms. The district and municipal action systems, the advisory services in the fisheries and others, could function as catalysts. But only those that are part of the network—the firms—can provide the trust.

Working Smarter 6

The Coastal Expertise Committee envisages a future in which the fish processing industry will become the "marine food industry." This will require firms which utilize the latest in biotechnology, information technology and modern mariculture, and which are based on how the market functions. To achieve this, a change from present practice will be necessary. The Committee insists that there must be a radical increase in expertise in the firms and its 1990 submission to the government suggests a number of measures to implement change.

New opportunities for education within the fish processing industry and fish farming are suggested. Bursaries would make it possible to send experts to the firms or to send firm personnel to an external technical environment. The Committee also favours bursaries for visits to countries which import Norwegian products, in order to create greater market orientation in the firms. Training of vocational teachers in fisheries subjects must be improved and new teaching methods developed. It is also suggested that the system of issuing trade papers be further developed to include all links in the industry.

WASTED EFFORT?

When considering the challenges the industry is faced with, such measures should be implemented and welcomed. In certain circumstances, however, any increase in experience may be a wasted effort. The experience so far gained in the fish processing industry, particularly the so-called OIF-projects,[1] shows that it cannot be taken for granted that education leads to change in all circumstances (see Henriksen 1990; Myhra and Langli 1988).

Figure 1

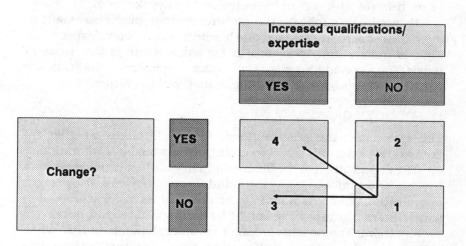

Certain organizational forms appear to reduce the probability that increased expertise will result in change. Organizational development will therefore often be essential in order for increased knowledge and expertise to result in change and development. The problem can be expressed as follows, using the four-field table shown above.

If we say we are in square 1, that is, low expertise and therefore no change, the assumption is that engaging in education and training will bring us to square 4. However, the table shows that there are also other possibilities. For example, one could risk ending up in square 3. Here, increased expertise is tried, but that does not lead to change. Everyone in the firm becomes more knowledgable, but it has no effect on their behaviour in the firm or the firm's behaviour in the marketplace. Instead, everything remains the same.

We may end up in square 2. Here, changes occur without any increase in expertise. This is a situation where the firm employs new technology or goes into new markets without being properly equipped with expertise. The firm is therefore not ready to learn from its experience. It is in a very shaky position, and risks no return on its investment. It is also possible to end up with one foot in square 2 and one in square 3. That is the case when changes take place without an increase in expertise being the cause. Training measures may be irrelevant in the face of changes in the surroundings to which the firm must respond. This, too, is a situation where the firm would be on thin ice with regard to controlling its development.

To further complicate the picture, change may also result in increased expertise, provided one learns from one's own experience. That is mainly how increases in expertise occur in the industry today. The Coastal Expertise Committee is convinced that this will not be good enough in the fishing industry of the future.

INTROVERTED ORGANIZATION

The claim that the organizational form determines whether increased expertise will result in change needs further elaboration.

The organization of the fishing industry is often considered from a rights and conflict perspective—and for good reasons. The present organizational pattern is mainly the result of an historic process in which interest groups have fought for their special rights, or tried to protect them. The process has had an inner dynamic in that when one group has organized itself, its opponent or competitor has done the same for defensive reasons. The result is not just a flowering of organizations, but also an "extroverted" industry with "introverted" organization, as formulated by Hallenstvedt (1982). We have, then, an industry which fights its biggest battles with itself, which uses too much time and energy on internal conflicts and distribution matters and too little time on increasing the industry's total returns.

An industry organized to promote interests is not at the same time automatically organized to promote learning and development of expertise. An industry which wants to attract expertise, which cares about it and gets it to bloom, must also be organized accordingly. First and foremost, it must ensure that the expertise will be used when important decisions are made. This is related to the connection between research and industrial activity among other things. Secondly, incentives must be structured so that it pays for the firms and those involved in the industry to engage in building up expertise. In the previous chapter it was maintained that industrial organizations weaken the build-up of market expertise on a business level. Thirdly, it is necessary to ensure that expertise also flows down to the small and scattered local units.

It is not a foregone conclusion that all the expertise should be built up in a single plant. Some expertise could more effectively be developed on a higher organizational level, for example, in trade organizations. Local plants can also join together for recruiting and building up expertise. Expertise is an expensive production factor but, at the same time, it can be divided without being diminished. In fact, it grows by being shared with others. The new things one learns can be added to old knowledge, and the knowledge one then has can be returned in a refined state.

COMPLEXITY

The relationship between organization, increased expertise and change can best be demonstrated on a business level. There are certain ways of organizing businesses which promote learning and adaptability to change. Much of the literature on organizational theory is devoted to this subject. MacDonald (1988) has presented a useful figure to illustrate the relationship between changes in the firm's surroundings and technology on the one hand, and the firm's internal organization on the other (see Figure 2). Technological complexity, which follows the vertical axis in the diagram, deals with, among other things, how fast the technology is developing and the degree of uncertainty about how it works. This complexity also applies to the knowledge required to utilize the technology. MacDonald is of the opinion that fish farming exemplifies an industry characterized by high technological complexity: it is new, the technology is constantly developing, and it is not always possible to predict results and problems (disease, for example).

Figure 2

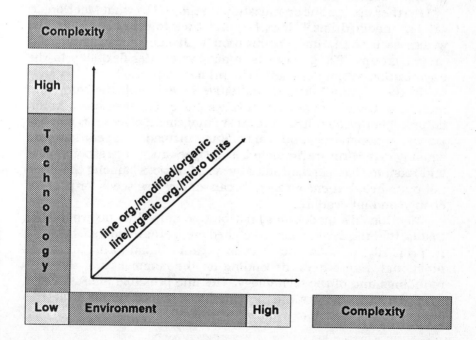

The complexity of the environment along the horizontal axis concerns, among other things, the number of external factors the firm is dependent on and how conflicting and diffuse are the expectations with which it is faced. Complexity also depends on how fast the environment changes and how much information about the surroundings the firm needs in order to to take appropriate action.

The ability of a firm to control the challenges along both axes depends to a great degree on its expertise. The two axes can also be regarded as time axes. Both technology and environment have steadily become more complex over the years and have resulted in an increased need for greater expertise. If export and marketing of fish products were decentralized, as opposed to the present situation, the firms would have their fingers on the pulse of the market. This would lead to a dramatic increase in the complexity of the environment that they would have to deal with and that, again, would make it necessary to increase expertise.

FUNCTIONAL ORGANIZATION

Along the diagonal in the diagram, MacDonald hooks in various forms of organization. At the bottom, where technology, as well as the environment, are simple, we find the line organization, that is, an organization with a hierarchical structure characterized by strict division of labour and a clear chain of command and responsibility.

Further up, the line organization is replaced by what MacDonald calls a "modified line." Here, the firm tries to compensate for the weaknesses of the line organization with staff departments and project groups. The purpose is to achieve greater flexibility in the organization without changing the primary structure.

In the "organic" firm, a qualitative breach with the command method of the line organization takes place. The firm has a much flatter organizational structure and management places less emphasis on commanding and controlling. Instead, cooperation and equality in the firm are promoted. Employees are given responsibility and room for independent initiatives. "Mavericks" among them are not punished, but encouraged, because they sow seeds for positive change and innovation.

MacDonald's model must not be understood as deterministic, that is, that the development sketched out is unavoidable. The point is, primarily, to show that certain organizational forms are more functional than others, depending on the complexity of the surroundings and of the technology. The line principle is best suited when the surroundings and the technology remain simple, while the organic is best suited to complex situations.

LAGGING BEHIND

Increased complexity does not automatically result in a transition from a line to an organic organization. In practice, there will often be a considerable lag. The firm's organizational form will lag behind in relation to the changes in the environment. This is due to many factors, for example, a lack of expertise. The transition from line to organic organization also means equalization of power in the firm. People in key positions may feel that their positions are threatened, and react by throwing a monkey wrench into the works.

It may be that the market mechanism reduces this lag in that only the most adaptable firms will survive. Even if this happens in some industries, however, it does not necessarily happen in all. Industries are more or less exposed to competition. Some are also backed by the state. It is therefore quite possible for an industry or branch with high technological and environmental complexity to consist of firms organized according to the line principle. The fish processing industry is becoming a good example of this.

The Coastal Expertise Committee believes that the fish processing industry will become an "intelligent industry," that is, an industry based on advanced technology and knowledge. If the goal is to become a marine food industry, new trails must be broken, and chances taken on new technology and new markets. This will put the firms into more complex situations. It is then paradoxical that most of the modern fish processing plants in Norway slavishly follow Frederick Taylor's classic Scientific Management ideas. The most technologically advanced firms use assembly line technology, thereby reducing jobs to the simplest manual operations. They use computer technology for more detailed supervision of the work.

EARLY DEATH

If the most competent and creative employees perceive the organizational form of their firm as frustrating and obstructive, then, according to MacDonald, there is a danger of their leaving the firm, preferably to go out on their own. When they don't get the elbow room they need within the line-organized firm, the result is often that they break loose and establish an "organic micro-unit," as indicated in the diagram.

It is not necessarily a bad thing that creative employees go out on their own. This may create dynamism in the branch. New gains have often come out of such moves. The old firm loses by losing a worker, but the industry and the community gain by the establishment of a new firm.

In other respects there are drawbacks. New firms are often fragile and the probability of failure is high. Figures for Norwegian industry published in *Dagens Næringsliv* (2 April 1991) show that 17 percent of the firms that declared bankruptcy in 1990 were less than one year old, while 60 percent were under five years old.

Some new firms probably fail quickly because the product idea was not sound, or the firm lacked sufficient financial resources. But sometimes the reason is insufficient expertise. Often the entrepreneur has expertise along only one of the axes in the diagram. The tendency may also be that the higher the expertise an entrepreneur possesses along the one axis in the diagram, the more inclined he or she is to underestimate the challenges along the other axis.

Thus there is a danger of good product ideas being lost to society. It is likely that they could have been realized within the firm where the entrepreneur was originally employed if the internal organizational prerequisites had been appropriate. The challenge therefore consists in creating organizations which consider creative "mavericks" a resource and not a threat. It is important to set up reward systems which extend to the whole firm and stimulate, not frustrate, creative employees.

INDUSTRIAL DEMOCRACY

Experiments with expertise development in the fish processing industry (through the previously mentioned OIF projects) indicate that something must be done with the organization of plants if training measures are to be effective. Employees who have taken training courses come home full of enthusiasm and ideas for improvement of the routines but often meet with scepticism and lack of enthusiasm, particularly at the middle management level. Some of the plants which participated in the projects have since taken steps to change the line organization by establishing so-called training committees in which the employees are in charge while upper and middle managers are ordinary members.

When arguing for greater worker influence in the plants, the focus is often on interest, power and income distribution. The OIF projects, however, show that industrial democracy can also be discussed from a perspective of change in which greater influence by workers is a prerequisite for increased expertise to be converted to growth and development. Without industrial democracy, there is a risk of an exodus of skill. If increased expertise is considered an investment for the purpose of earning income for the plant, the employees must also be allowed to utilize the plant to realize their own goals, not just the goals set by management.

Work to Live   7

Industrial fish processing is mainly a post-war phenomenon. In the 1950s and 1960s, a large modern fish processing industry based on freezing and the trawl fishery was established with great public input. Small receiver plants with little processing of the product became more technologically advanced; they began to produce brand-name products and created considerable employment in the processing link. The fisheries statistics for 1990 show that about 10,000 people were employed in the fish processing industry, all types of production included. The fish processing industry is therefore very significant to employment along the coast. The crisis in the fishing industry hits not only a large number of fishermen, but the fish plant workers as well.

WORK FOR WOMEN

The fish processing industry has given women in the coastal communities, in particular, opportunities for paid work. The study for The Coastal Expertise Committee (mentioned in previous chapters), found that women workers were in the majority in 20 percent of the North Norwegian fish processing plants. Few of them work full time. In one out of three plants, more than half of the women are part-time employees. Many are wives of fishermen; in such households the crisis hits both sources of income.

Unstable supplies of raw material have been common in the fish processing industry through the years, with the resultant uncertainty in employment. In 1985, which was not a crisis year, only 30 percent of North Norwegian fish processing plants operated without temporary shutdowns. Frequent lay-offs combined with generally low wage levels and poor work environments have given the fish processing industry a bad name. Nowadays, a job in the fish processing industry has a low status.

In many localities, the plants have difficulty in recruiting and keeping their work force even if there is high unemployment in the area. Young people, in particular, consider a job in a fish plant as temporary. Many apply for these jobs only because there are no other alternatives available, and leave the plant as soon as they can find other work. Some parents threaten their children that unless they do well in school they will end up on the filleting line.

Such problems will not disappear when the fish resources return to normal levels. The problems were there before the crisis came and will not disappear when there is enough fish. Now is the time to look at job enrichment in the fish processing industry, even though some problems may appear more pressing.

MONOTONOUS WORK

Personnel policy has a great deal to do with how attractive jobs in the fish processing industry are; and with how the firms invest in their employees and to what degree they arrange for training and personal development in their work. Certainly, the product, the production process and the available technology limit the content of the job. To stand by a conveyor belt or a filleting machine is monotonous at best, despite frequent breaks and a friendly atmosphere. There is, however, considerable scope for providing the jobs with qualitatively better content than they have today.

Several measures are appropriate. Training could make the job more interesting; greater job rotation would reduce monotony and stress injuries, and the wage system could be made less stressful. Better information to the employees could reduce the job uncertainty that many experience, and could help the workers to see the firm from a broader perspective than is visible from their work station. Joint decision-making could reduce the arbitrariness workers often experience and help to develop and create loyalty. Further processing produces more finished products, and entails knowledge and skill on the part of workers. Who can be happy in a job where no such opportunities exist?

An active personnel policy requires resources—it is expensive to invest in training, welfare and improvements to the work environment. Furthermore, management often considers joint decision-making as interference, and dissemination of information to employees a waste of time, a luxury that in times of crisis they can ill afford. But perhaps it is precisely at such times that one should invest in such ventures, as some fish processing plants are already doing.

It is difficult to show a correlation between good personnel policies and the profitability of a firm. Even though management may see the benefit of such measures, it may be difficult to estimate how far they should go. There is also doubt about the wisdom of investing in the development of personnel because expertise is an asset that can be sold to competing firms.

Modern management theory insists that a good personnel policy is a good investment. According to our studies of North Norwegian fish plants, it appears that managers are not convinced. Only 24 percent of managers answered that a good work environment is among the three most important factors required to ensure profitability; 17 percent said that technical expertise is one of the most important, while 71 percent emphasized that the quantity produced is one of the three most important factors contributing to profitability.

In a later study of personnel management in the fish processing industry, we looked at ten different firms and asked the managers for, among other things, their views on the importance of investing in personnel development.[1] The answers varied widely.

RESOURCEFULNESS

There are managers who feel that welfare and other personnel policy measures are the reasons for many bankruptcies in the fish processing industry and who are therefore satisfied to meet the bare minimum requirements required by law and collective agreements. Other fish plant managers think quite differently. They have ambitious goals for personnel policy and invest heavily to meet certain absolute and self-imposed standards—wages and work environment must be as good as possible! Full employment is a goal, even in times of scarcity of raw material!

Resourcefulness is displayed in personnel policy, not only in recruiting a work force, but also in creating a positive work environment. Many managers encourage their workers to make suggestions for improvements in the work environment by establishing their own suggestion and development committees. In one plant, they hold "coffee meetings" to inform the employees about the operation and future plans. A company newspaper has been started in which the workers can speak out anonymously. The same plant has also started a day care centre, and even holds dances to increase satisfaction among its employees. This management considers the expenses insignificant in relation to what they get back, although the returns cannot be measured in money. A full 72 percent of the employees said they were happy in their jobs, while only 3 percent

expressed dissatisfaction. This is high compared to other plants
included in the study.

Some managers consider a personnel policy to be an opportun-
istic means of recruiting workers. Personnel benefits are heavily
market-dependent; they are made more attractive when there is a
shortage of workers and less so when there is a good supply. Thus
there is a great variation over time and between plants in how
investments in personnel benefits are made. Other managers see a
personnel policy as a yoke which forces them to maintain a level of
employment that the supply of raw material or the market situation
does not support. One manager said:

> A temporary lay-off of personnel would often be more profitable
> than producing for storage or buying expensive raw material to
> keep the wheels turning, as we are doing. In other words, we are
> not producing in the most profitable manner from a market point
> of view. This is expensive in the short term. Raw material storage
> ties up capital, but in the long run it is more costly to lay people
> off. Skills are forgotten and the plant loses its efficiency. It creates
> negative feelings toward industrial work and frustration among the
> employees.

Nevertheless, when there are no supplies of raw material, lay-offs
are difficult to avoid. They are so common in the fish processing
industry that only three days' notice is given, while in the rest of the
economy two weeks' notice is required. Even so, plants try to avoid
lay-offs by attempting to equalize the flow of raw material. The study
of the North Norwegian fish plants cited earlier showed that almost
70 percent actively tried to stabilize employment by double freezing,
further processing, long-term storage of live fish and purchase of
raw material from other plants.

IMPLICIT PERSONNEL POLICY

If one asks a plant manager what his personnel policy is, a straight
answer is not always forthcoming. Only the largest fish plants have
their own personnel department and can refer to written goals. One
large plant had as an official goal, "to create good and stable work
places for the employees . . . work to increase the employees' motivation and feeling of belonging in the plant, and actively seeking to
develop a positive plant culture."

In smaller plants, the personnel function is just one of the many
tasks the manager looks after on a daily basis. Like other management tasks, it is carried out in an informal manner. This does not
necessarily mean that it is done with arbitrariness or indifference to
the employees; rather, the personnel policy is included as a matter

of course and is an integral part of everyday management practice. It is implicit and is only evident in how the plant treats its employee on an everyday basis.

When the personnel policy is not in writing or is not the object of conscious planning on the part of management, it may easily acquire a character of what psychologists call "rationalization," by which it becomes a matter of interpretation and depends on the manager's understanding of how it is to be applied. It ceases to be a guide for consistent action, and becomes instead a defence of what is necessary and opportune at any given time.

There are often different interpretations of what a firm's personnel policy really is. Management and employees have different ideas of what the policy intends and what its effects are. The employees will find that there is not always agreement between theory and practice—between what management says and what it does. In our study we found cases where management thought that the employees were satisfied with the policy, while the employees themselves reported considerable frustration and resignation.

One manager we interviewed stated that "a good personnel policy is one where the people are satisfied with their jobs." The employees stated that "a good personnel policy is one where there is good contact between management and employees." The workers had a more concrete idea of what is required.

ABSENTEEISM

In recent years the fish processing industry has invested considerable amounts of money in upgrading the physical working conditions in the plants. Structural improvements have made draughts, cold and noise less of a problem than before. New machinery has eliminated heavy lifting. But the fish processing industry is still plagued by high absenteeism due to illness. Some plants in our study had nearly half the work force absent at one time. Repetitious and monotonous work is speeded up by automation, and piecework must also take some of the blame for absenteeism.

The piecework system, by which workers are paid according to the amount done, is controversial for many reasons. Not only may it be injurious to health, but the injuries may also be kept private. In principle, the employee is free to set his/her own pace, but in practice it is difficult to reduce the output because the wage level is low, particularly on a yearly basis, and because it could easily affect one's co-workers. Piecework also contributes to competition between employees. This may be good for efficiency but it creates wage differences which make it difficult to agree on which wage system is preferable. It weakens the team spirit which forms the basis for a common front in the face of management.

The large turnover in the work force does not make the situation any better. Many take only a short-sighted view of their job—that they are there only for the season, and it is a matter of working as hard as possible. For those who are permanently employed and who have been there for a long time, the outlook is different. For them, the tempo becomes a health problem after a while.

Changes in the wage system are often discussed in the plants. Both in management and among the employees, there are different opinions as to what a change from piecework to hourly wages would entail. Some feel it would lower efficiency and the firms cannot afford that. For the workers, it could mean a reduced income and that is a risk many are not willing to take. Others feel that with hourly wages the quality of the product would be better because haste would be reduced. A female fish plant worker who depended on hourly wages stated:

> Better work is done with a good hourly wage. Efficiency will not be reduced. Piecework doesn't make people more efficient, because you can only work in 'high gear' in spurts. Hourly wages with a more even work speed is better. You would then reduce absentee-ism due to ill health. With such a wage system, the plants would also obtain a better product and would gain in the long run. Today, everyone is trying to earn as much as possible and quality suffers accordingly.

Occupational injuries are a significant problem in the fish proc-essing industry, whether due to the wage system, the monotonous work or the production equipment. The difficulty in determining which of the three factors is of greatest significance has not pre-vented some of the plants in our study from dispensing with piece-work. One of the plants permits individual workers to elect hourly wages or piecework pay.

Another measure adopted by several plants is job rotation. We found examples in our study of workers themselves taking the initiative for such an arrangement. They have not managed to create rotation between male and female jobs, though, so job variation is not as great as it might have been. The women have the most monotonous work and suffer the most strain. The lack of rotation between male and female jobs also contributes to injuries because strain and absenteeism are considered female problems, rather than a problem of the production method.

SEX MYTHS

No one who visits a fish processing plant can fail to notice the distribution of work by sexes. The women are in the filleting hall busily clean-cutting, weighing and packaging, while the men are in the other departments—on the wharf, in the cutting hall, in the freezing and cooling plant, in the finished product department, and definitely in management. The women are assigned to routine work and to operations requiring the least skill.

Why this type of work distribution? Why don't we see men equipped with tweezers looking for bones in fillets? Why do we rarely see a woman forklift operator?

Marit Husmo and Eva Munk-Madsen (1989) at the Norwegian College of Fishery Science (Norges Fiskerihøgskole) questioned management and employees in the fish processing industry about this. How do they justify the sex division? The answers they received were that women and men are best suited for different tasks. Women are dexterous, clean, accurate, quick and, above all, patient. This makes them suitable for trimming the fillets. Men are physically stronger, have technical insight, are more conscious of responsibility and more stable. This makes them qualified for more varied and demanding tasks; they are needed in many places in the plant. They are better suited than women to operate machinery, drive forklifts and, not least, to supervise.

Husmo and Munk-Madsen call these ideas "sex myths." Sex myths block the way to a more even distribution of the work because that is regarded as a breach of "the natural order." Women are therefore not given an opportunity to show that they are capable of doing other tasks. Nor are they given an opportunity to develop skills for other jobs. Instead, they are locked into the work which is ranked low in the plant. This is in the interest of the men, who are strong in defence of their own positions with the support of sex myths. It does not help that the women themselves often accept the sex myths as an explanation of the distribution of the work. For women, men's jobs therefore become an inconceivable step up in the organization. For men, women's jobs are a degrading step downwards.

Husmo and Munk-Madsen maintain that changes in sex distribution rarely happen spontaneously. More is needed than for a woman to demonstrate that she can handle a man's job. She will not necessarily be accepted as proof that "women can do it!" The sex myths are rigid and such a breach of the rules is easy to explain away. The same happens when a new machine makes a man's work physically lighter and therefore within the range of women's capabilities. Then the emphasis is placed on technical insight, another purported male quality.

Greater mixing of the sexes therefore depends on "strategic personnel management." It is not in the power of management to do away with sex myths in one fell swoop, but they can do something about the distribution of work and thereby also attack the myths. Systematic job rotation where women are assigned to "men's" jobs, and vice versa, may result in shaking the myths. Technical training of women may produce a similar effect.

NEGOTIATING STRENGTH

Since women are often in the majority in the plants, one would think that it would be possible to force changes. But the women in the coastal districts do not have many job opportunities outside the fish processing industry. As housewives, they are also bound to the locality and must limit themselves to part-time employment. Therefore, their negotiating position is weak. They cannot dictate a minimum price, as the fishermen can under the Raw Fish Act. They are often the first to be laid off when the raw material supply or the market fails.

Until now, higher qualifications and years of experience have not been regarded as important to a job in the fish processing industry. The only thing required is "a willingness to work and a good disposition," as it was stated in a job advertisement from one large plant. People with theoretical and practical qualifications often have expectations which the plant cannot, or will not, meet. In such plants, the workers rarely remain long in the job, according to some managers in our study.

There are certain conditions which appear to strengthen the women's negotiating position. The recruitment base is limited and the plant depends on the local population. Women can achieve advantages in the form of "housewives' shifts" and flex time. Such arrangements are about to become common in the fish processing industry.

Many fish plants depend on migrant workers. In addition to local workers, there are often people from the outside on short-term visits. In recent years, the influx of foreign workers—Finns and Tamils— has been considerable, and the work force has become quite mixed. Sometimes this leads to poor communication and poor team spirit. It does not help that the migrant workers are often housed in apartments separate from the local population.

Another consequence is that the plant will have to adapt its personnel policy to a very heterogeneous work force. It is difficult to implement a standardized personnel policy which would treat everyone equally. Special considerations are not without problems. Different treatment of workers based on their various needs and problems can easily be interpreted as preferential treatment. The foundation for conflict is then laid.

TRADE UNIONS

This potential conflict presents a challenge to the unions which, in many plants, are active participants in the personnel policy. Close to 80 percent of all fish plant workers belong to a union. This is a high proportion which, admittedly, varies between large and small plants. There are certain advantages to being a member, for instance, three days' notice is required before one can be laid off. The Norwegian Food and Allied Workers Union (Norsk Nærings-og Nytelsesmiddel-arbeiderforbund) which organizes all fish plant workers, has collective agreements with 300 of the 450 fish plants.

Our study found that the activity of the union varies considerably. In some plants, the union is aggressive and enjoys great support among the work force. In other plants, there is little activity, and when meetings are called hardly anyone shows up. We found instances of management having to take the initiative in the election of shop stewards.

There are times when it is difficult to talk openly about personnel policy, particularly for someone who is at the bottom of the ladder and a migrant worker. The union is therefore important. It makes the personnel policy a formal matter of which a person can speak as a representative instead of as an individual. It is then easier to conduct direct discussions.

The union also contributes to routine contact with management. Meetings are held regularly, rules are established for matters to be presented and information is exchanged. In other words, it averts the situation one worker described: "Often we stand there and egg each other on until we explode." Regularized communication and rules should reduce complaints like that of the worker who said, "Nowadays the manager approaches various people depending on what is the matter. It looks as if he selects cooperative people depending on the situation."

Informal contacts between management and employees do have their positive side. They may form the basis for vertically reliable, trusting and supportive relations in the plant. An employee's remark about one manager—"He is one of us. He is no white collar and we know him so well"—reveals good communication and good treatment of personnel.

JOB QUALITY

We not only work to live, we also live to work; the quality of our work contributes to the quality of our lives. There is every reason to be interested in the content of the jobs offered people in the fish processing industry.

A restored raw material base will bring the jobs back again. That is important and necessary, but we should be more ambitious than that. The workers must consider a job in the fish processing industry as meaningful and, for this to occur, the quality of jobs must be improved. Otherwise people's interest in work in the fish processing industry will be, at best, temporary. This will hurt not only the fish processing industry but also the local communities in which it is situated because people will move out of the area.

Is Resettlement the Answer?   8

Why are people moving away from the fishing districts? Why are there continually fewer and fewer making their living from the traditional coastal industries? Why do the young people leave?

Such questions have been a theme of the social debate for the last 25 years. It is widely believed that we face a serious problem and that it is a public responsibility to rectify it. There has been disagreement regarding the concrete goals and means, but there is no disagreement about the need to stem the flow of outmigration and to counter trends towards centralization.

That the settlement pattern has not been consolidated may be blamed on the failure of the regional policy.[1] Maybe the dosage of the medicine was wrong or not strong enough. The medicine itself may have been wrong—maybe other means should have been used. Or perhaps the diagnosis itself was misleading, and the causes of the departures have been misunderstood.

The District Committee, which presented its report in 1984 (NOU 1984:21A), was very critical of the district-by-district effect of transferring income to agriculture and fisheries. This may indicate that the medicine is the root cause, even if no one can complain about the dosage. If the millions in subsidies passed out to the district industries over the years were added up, the amount would be staggering. This indicates a need for a new diagnosis.

WHAT DO WE BELIEVE?

The complexity of the outmigration problem should not be underestimated. It is difficult to identify all the causes of past and present outmigration. Perhaps people today move for different reasons than they did before. In earlier times, the lack of work led to outmigration.

Today, it may be the quality of the jobs that is the problem. Perhaps the jobs available in the coastal districts are not attractive enough?

In order to understand why people leave the coast, perhaps one should ask, who is leaving? It is not a foregone conclusion that various population groups, be it youth, people with education, women, or families, move as much and for the same reasons. There are probably many different reasons why people leave. Single-factor explanations will probably not contribute much. Perhaps many conditions must come together at the same time, and outmigration becomes the solution when the "cup runneth over."

To further complicate the picture, it may be that outmigration is a chain reaction in which one problem gives rise to the next. The District Committee put forward one such explanation when it stated:

> Women have had the greatest difficulty in finding work in the outport communities and have moved out at a very young age. On the one hand, this has resulted in villages being left with many unmarried (men) and, on the other hand, has caused the men to move after (the women).

> Because the girls move, the boys move too. If this analysis is correct, then the outmigration should be easy to stop. All that is needed is to do something with the first link in the chain, and the rest will solve itself. In other words, if something is done for the girls, the boys will stay.

In Norway, we generally have great belief in such chain reaction explanations. For example, it has been taken for granted that the settlement problems in the coastal communities would have to be solved through the fishing industry. The fisheries create a lot of spin-off activities, and if only the supplies of raw material were secured, then the outmigration problem would be solved automatically. But this model is unrealistic for the future. More than a stable supply of raw material is needed. It is, strangely enough, not only the weakest fishing communities which have difficulties in hanging on to their girls. In the 1980s, the young women also left the strongest and most expansive fishing communities.

It will hardly suffice to direct the effort to the first link in the chain of causes, since there are many causes which act independently of each other and chains are interlocked. Moreover—to return to a medical metaphor—even if we find the right medication, there is always a risk of side effects.

DILEMMA

The district policy is full of dilemmas and "tragic" choices. They can be found, not least, in the fishing industry, where measures to achieve efficiency and increased profitability may also lessen opportunities for decentralization and geographic spread of the activities. It is difficult to maximize economic efficiency and employment at the same time. In the fishing industry we have experienced a drastic reduction in the number of fishermen—from 115,000 in 1946 to around 25,000 today—without this having affected the harvesting capacity.

This great increase in productivity has led to concentration of population. The same has occurred in agriculture—making it more effective reduced the population of the villages. In agriculture, the market has put a cap on growth; in the fishing industry, it is the fish resources which are the main limiting factor. With such shackles, increased efficiency has been at the expense of employment, and the scattered settlements have suffered accordingly.

WHAT DO WE WANT?

The negative relationships between efficiency, employment and decentralized settlements have forced many to conclude that outmigration is not only unavoidable, but necessary in order to achieve growth and development, and that outmigration and areas of greater population density are actually desirable.

To transfer employment from "low-productivity" primary industries to "high-productivity" secondary and tertiary industries was a clear goal of the North Norway plan of 1952. The North Norway Regional Committee (Landsdelskomiteen for Nord Norge) of the 1970s wanted to stem the tide of outmigration, not by freezing the settlement pattern, but by channelling the flow in to towns and densely populated areas —"growth centres" as the Committee called them. "Continued changes in industrial and settlement structure are necessary prerequisites for positive development of North Norway," said the Committee.

The proposal caused dissension. Municipal boards and provincial councils were strongly against the proposed growth centres, and today the concept is no longer part of the regional policy debate. Yet the idea of directing resettlement to certain selected densely populated areas is far from dead.

The authorities thus appear to have an indecisive and ambivalent outlook on the outmigration problem. Outmigration is both desirable and undesirable, and is regarded as something necessary and unavoidable. This mixed view has led to rather imprecise goals in the district policy. The objective stated in public planning documents—"to maintain the main features of our present settlement pattern"—is ambiguous in light of the shifting patterns and inconsistent policy.

THE DOMINO EFFECT

If the authorities have a confused outlook on the causes of outmigration, that is partly because social science studies have not produced straightforward explanations for them. While most researchers agree that outmigration from fishing districts is related to developments in the fisheries, there is disagreement about the nature and consequences of the process.

What happens in a fishing community, for example, when the number of fishermen is reduced? Will the remaining fishermen be better or worse off? The questions go right to the core of fisheries economic theory. The answer will determine one's position on whether a decline in the number of fishermen is an advantage or a problem requiring public action.

Most fisheries economists think that the fewer fishermen the better. The reasoning should be remembered from Chapter 3: since the fishermen tax the resources of the commons, there is a tendency to overpopulation. From an economic point of view, there are too many fishermen and too much capital involved in the industry. This leads to increased competition and decreased profitability. With fewer participants, the competition is reduced and the remainder will get more fish to share. A decrease in the number of fishermen would contribute to an increase in profitability and stabilize employment in the industry, both for the industry as a whole and for individual participants.

What, then, would be the other side of the coin? Could it be worse, rather than better, for the remaining fishermen when they are fewer in number? Perhaps a reduction in participation means that the local fishing community is disintegrating. (This is also an argument in the Norwegian agriculture debate.) As discussed in Chapter 3, the fishermen are not only competitors, they are dependent on each other and cooperate extensively. This indicates that a decrease in the number of fishermen could have negative consequences. It may be like falling dominos: one drags the others down with it.

If one believes that the remaining fishermen would be better off if they were fewer, then one is embracing the consolidation theory; if one assumes that their situation would be worse, one subscribes to the domino theory. These theories reflect various opinions of what a fishing society looks like from a strictly social viewpoint. In the first case, it is assumed that the social relationships are marked by competition and conflicting interests; in the second, it is assumed that the relationships are primarily symbiotic in nature, that the fishermen mutually benefit from each other.

VULNERABLE FISHING COMMUNITIES

The domino theory holds that a fisheries-dependent community is vulnerable, particularly in periods of depression. It is the social and economic systems which collapse. Once the downward spiral has started, it will tend to be self-reinforcing. If we wanted to study the changes in the number of fishermen, we would expect to find a descending curve which became constantly steeper. According to the consolidation theory, on the other hand, this process could be expected to stop by itself and the curve would flatten out when the "right" number of fishermen had been reached.

Some years ago I tried to study the validity of these theories using public statistics (Jentoft 1984). I found that many fishing communities had a dramatic drop in the number of fishermen in the period 1973 to 1983.

Among all the fishing municipalities, Dønna had the most dramatic decrease, having lost half of its fishermen during that 10-year period. During the '60s, Dønna had one of the country's strongest purse seine fleets; and the drop in the number of fishermen reflected the collapse of this fleet.

Vardø experienced a similar development. Here, a group of very active long liners disappeared. In addition, municipalities such as Bjarkøy, Gildeskål, Steigen and Lurøy fared very poorly. Fishing municipalities on the West Coast (Vestlandet) such as Sund, Kvitsøy and Fedje, also experienced abnormal losses of fishermen during this period. In Trøndelag province, Frøya experienced a large drop in the number of fishermen.

Donna and Vardø were not the only municipalities to depend on one type of fishing; Bjarkøy used to have an active long liner fleet. In Lurøy, there had been a productive group of seiners in addition to some large boats long-lining on Trænabanken during the '60s. And in Fedje, whale and basking shark hunting had been very important.

The domino theory does not say anything about what triggers such downward processes, only what causes them to accelerate once they get started. In some districts, the trigger may have been a new bridge connection which made commuting possible, or the oil activity that suddenly became an alternative to fishing. When some fishermen quit, others followed suit.

There are many things besides the domino effect which could explain the slump. We have previously mentioned that when the women move, the men move also. Ageing may be another factor. Or income may be so low that nobody can make a living off the fishery. I took these factors into account in my study, and found that they could explain only part of the decline in those districts which lost the most fishermen during this period. Attempts to weaken the domino theory actually ended up strengthening it.

THE TOP TEN

There is not necessarily a correlation between the decline in the number of fishermen and outmigration from the fishing districts. The fishermen who stop fishing may have found other work locally or within commuting distance. A study by Bjørn Hersoug (1985) at the Norwegian College of Fishery Science (Norges Fiskerihøgskole) found that 55 percent of the fishermen registered in 1971 had changed employment or dropped out of the work force between 1971 and 1980. Of these, only 11 percent had moved to other districts and only 3 percent had moved out of the province. Changes in occupation resulted in only a modest number moving. He drew the conclusion that, in the '70s, the fishermen, by staying in the community, contributed to consolidation of the settlement pattern.

An increase in the number of fishermen does not always indicate stabilization of a settlement. Vestvågøy is a good example: few other fishing municipalities experienced such positive development during the 1970s and 1980s, but the population as a whole still decreased through outmigration.

Even in districts which show the greatest loss of fishermen *and* the greatest outmigration, it is not always the fishermen who move. The table below provides some insight. It shows the 10 fishing municipalities with the largest outmigration and the greatest decrease in the numbers of fishermen in the '80s. Only Røst, Skjervøy and Måsøy appear in both groups, that is, among the ten communities with both the greatest decrease in the number of fishermen and the largest net outmigration. This may indicate a certain correlation. However, the correlation coefficient—the statistical measure for the degree of covariation, in this case between the decrease in the number of fishermen and net outmigration—almost equals zero. Thus, there is very little to indicate that the municipalities which had the greatest drop in the number of fishermen during the period 1983–1986 also had the greatest net outmigration.

Hasvik municipality illustrates: it is in third place on the "top ten" list of municipalities with the greatest net outmigration but, at the same time, the municipality had the greatest increase in the number of fishermen during the period 1983 to 1986. The increase was a full 25 percent. Træna municipality is in almost the same situation; high net outmigration (1.8 percent), but large growth (11 percent) in the number of fishermen.[2]

Table 4 Fishing municipalities with the largest outmigration and the greatest decrease in the numbers of fishermen in the 1980s

Average net outmigration 1980-86 in % of population figure for 1980		Reduction, number fishermen 1983-86 in % of total number sole or main income from fishing 1983	
Måsøy	2.54	Kvalsund	15.3
Flakstad	2.36	Måsøy	14.3
Hasvik	2.05	Torsken	13.8
Værøy	1.94	Herøy	13.7
Skjervøy	1.84	Kvitsøy	12.5
Røst	1.83	Karlsøy	11.9
Træna	1.81	Sandøy	9.9
Lebesby	1.67	Røst	9.4
Ibestad	1.64	Skjervøy	9.0
Berg	1.64	Austevoll	9.0

Source: Central Statistical Bureau of Norway and the Fishermen's Census (Norway).

WOMEN ARE LEAVING

If it is not the fishermen who move, then who is it? The answer is: the young women. The statistics say it in plain language. There is a shortage of women in the age group 20 to 39 years in all 36 municipalities which the Central Statistical Bureau of Norway classifies as fishing municipalities. In many of these municipalities, the shortage is considerable. The "top ten" list is presented below.

It is worth noting that the shortage of women is severe in both the North and the South, and that in most municipalities it increased in the 1980s, particularly in Finnmark province. It is also noteworthy that the only two fishing municipalities which showed greater immigration than outmigration in the 1980s, Austevoll and Øygarden, are among the municipalities having the greatest shortage of women. This weakens, if not nullifies, the hypothesis that the boys move because the girls do. Måsøy is the only municipality among the worst ten when it comes to net outmigration, decrease in the number of fishermen and low proportion of women.

Table 5   Fishing municipalities having greatest shortage of women

	Women, 20-39 years per 100 men, 1/1-1987	
	1987	1980
Solund	68	(65)
Kvalsund	73	(92)
Moskenes	75	(76)
Lurøy	76	(79)
Loppa	77	(79)
Torsken	78	(68)
Måsøy	79	(73)
Austevoll	79	(73)
Øygarden	79	(73)
Selje	79	(82)

Source: Central Statistical Bureau of Norway.

It is not something new that the young women move away from the districts. The figures which researcher Anne Grethe Flakstad (1987) has produced indicate that there are no more girls moving out now than there ever were. This has a greater impact on a settlement today, however, because families are now smaller. Now few women are left to start new families. A study from FORUT (Research Foundation, University of Tromsø) indicates that the annual increase in North Norway at the beginning of the 1970s was about 7,000 children; in 1987 it was about 2,000 (Nilsen 1987).

PARADOX

Traditionally, there have been few jobs available, outside of housework, for women in fishing communities. The fish processing industry was, by and large, the only employer. A significant improvement took place in the 1970s. The growth in the public sector, particularly in the "caring professions," such as teaching and nursing, produced both part-time and full-time jobs for many women. This, in turn, contributed to a certain consolidation of the settlement pattern. The caring professions also provided many young women with access to work, even though it was primarily the somewhat older women who were the first to be hired.

But now the growth in the public sector has stopped. Not many hospitals or day care centres are being built in the outlying districts, and those who were lucky enough to get jobs naturally prefer to hang on to them. So we are back to where we started from. The few jobs available are in the fish processing industry and it is being hit just as hard by the crisis as the fishermen themselves.

MORE DAYCARE CENTRES!

The work force in the fish processing industry consists mainly of two groups of women: quite young women and women of mature age with reduced responsibilities at home. Scattered reports indicate, however, that the entry of young women is decreasing. In that case, the fish processing industry is beginning to show a parallel with the ageing which is occurring in the fishing fleet in many districts.

There may be a number of reasons why so few young women are working in the fish processing industry. In the previous chapter we mentioned that the available jobs were not very attractive to women who have a choice. However, the reason need not be found only on the demand side of the labour market. There are few women with young families in the plants because they have problems combining work with child care. It is particularly difficult if the husband is a fisherman. When he is away, it is almost impossible to get away from the tasks at home.

Based on this, relief crewing[3] should be established and daycare centres are also needed. Daycare makes it possible to have a reasonable family life in which women can experience the satisfaction of having a job outside the home.

We have a long way to go until there are enough such opportunities in the fishing districts. Maybe the speeches made in favour of more child care centres during the 1988 parliamentary debate of the Fisheries Department budget signify a breakthrough.

Ground Crew 9

The coastal crisis has brought women into the fisheries policy arena as never before. They have stepped forward and insisted on what everybody should recognize: the crisis is not just about fishing regulations, over-capacity, adaptation of structure and failing profitability. It is also about the everyday lives of families, the dignity of people, and what to tell the young folks when what one has stood for and believed in no longer has any value.

Nobody knows for sure how long the crisis will last. It might be over by the middle of the '90s and it might last longer. However, fisheries policy would benefit from retaining the women's perspective when the times improve. The authorities hope that when that day comes we will be left with a leaner fishing industry, with fewer participants than the 25,000 fishermen who populate the coast today. The problem, as it is presented to the coastal population, is not that there will be fewer making their living from fishing, but that there are far too many of them today. The crisis may just generate the streamlining process which the authorities attempted, but which did not succeed, through buy-back of vessels and other structural measures.

"The menfolk look at their boats and equipment, while we look at the whole picture," said one participant at the annual meeting of Nordland Fishermen's Wives Association (Nordland Fiskarkvinnelag) (*Lofotposten* 19 September 1988). It is important that some one defend an overall perspective of an industry which, to a greater extent than most, is dominated by a fight over interests. The wives have to protect their own interests which so far, have been relegated to the background. There will be no vigorous local communities if the fisheries policy does not address the fishermen's wives directly. Their special interests are the theme of this chapter.

THE SINGLE MOTHER

The fishermen's wives share the fate of women whose husbands are working on the oil rigs or ply the oceans. They are single mothers with sole responsibility for home for long periods at a time. This daily burden does not become any lighter if she has a job outside the home. In addition, there is the radical change resulting from a father's coming and going. Studies of families in which the husbands work on the oil rigs or oceans show that this absence creates constant adjustment problems for the family (Solheim *et al.* 1986).

Oil workers and seamen have fixed job rhythms—they come home and leave on fixed schedules. The fisherman's working day, however, varies with the available fish and weather conditions. He must often leave on short notice and it is not easy to say when he will be home. The routine absence in the oil and seafaring industries makes it possible to have a structured family life. Everyday activities can be planned. In the fisherman's family, this is a far greater problem.

Fishermen are often absent for much longer periods than either oil workers or seafaring men; they may be away both winter and spring. Time studies from the end of the 1970s show that fishermen had almost double the working hours per annum compared to industrial workers (NOU 1980:22). These are working hours which are often spent so far away from home that they cannot get home in a day. Their leisure time must be spent either on board or in foreign ports.

FLEXIBILITY

A study of fishermen's wives' working days, which will be referred to in this chapter, has provided us with reasons to believe that a fisherman's family is faced with special challenges in many areas (Jentoft, ed. 1989).

First, irregular absences place great demands on the wife's flexibility. She must be able to improvise and plan on short notice, which forces her to allow safety margins and be prepared at all times. It also means that not all jobs are suitable for a fisherman's wife because many are hard to combine with responsibilities at home. A full-time job with fixed working hours can be too rigid for her, unless she has a special flex time arrangement with her employer.

To care for the children alone is a great responsibility and a considerable mental stress. The burden is increased in that fishing is one of our most dangerous occupations. The feeling of loneliness, combined with the worry about the person at sea, is a real strain for the women who were interviewed for our study. The strain on the nerves is not easily shared with others. The children, in particular, must be protected.

TRIPLE WORKERS

A third point is that a fisherman's wife participates in her husband's activities in a manner which separates her from other women. She looks after what Siri Gerrard (1983) calls "ground crew tasks." These are tasks such as line baiting, boat washing, accounting, purchasing spare parts, dealing with the bank, and so on. In other words, it is not only pilots who need ground support. In the fisheries, as opposed to aviation, it is the family, particularly the wife, who is ready when the boat touches shore. The ground crew role means that many fishermen's wives have not only two jobs like most working women, but three.

The result is a complementary and mutual dependency between husband and wife, both in the home and in professional life, which may create coordination problems on two fronts. The husband's and wife's jobs are often seasonal and at the same time of year. When the fishery is at its height and the greatest need is for the wife to be at home, there is at the same time a great demand for her labour as ground crew and as fish plant worker. This explains in part why the fish processing industry often has difficulty recruiting a local work force.

Sidsel Saugestad (1988) maintains that men's and women's work is ranked differently. The man's job takes precedence; the woman's has to adjust to his needs, not the reverse. In a fisherman's family there are special reasons for it to be that way. The ground crew tasks are determined by the rhythm of the fishery. A certain number of tubs must be baited before the boat leaves. Wives who have outside jobs, for example in the fish processing industry, also bring home income. The man, on the other hand, brings home a surplus if he owns a boat and equipment. In other words, his contribution to the family is that which is left over after expenses for boat and equipment have been deducted. If he takes a holiday, then it is not only the family's income which is lost, but also the income of the boat and crew.

ECONOMY OF LIFE

Jane Nadel-Klein and Dona Lee Davis (1988) point out that wives of fishermen have an important ideological task in making the fisheries an attractive occupation. Nadel-Klein and Davis maintain that, to the same degree as the men, the wives are "symbols of the fisher-man's occupation and the local community." The wife helps to strengthen the man's identity as a fisherman and to ensure new recruits, not only by giving birth to them, but also by giving them an outlook on life which is manifested in the fishing community.

Viggo Rossvær (1989) is also interested in the ideological func-tion of the wives of fishermen. In a study of the effects of the fishing crisis on a district in Finnmark, he points out that the traditional role of the wives of fishermen is to keep up courage and hope when everybody else has given up. "The wives not only keep the accounts for the boat, but also for life. She keeps account of the economy of life—it must produce a surplus and not a deficit." Rossvær has found that the present crisis has caused severe hardship for many wives in this regard.

ROLE CONFLICTS

Most fishermen wives, especially those employed outside the home, accept everyday role conflicts as unavoidable expenses, and try to live with them. For many, such employment is a step out of the loneliness and isolation, and it provides a feeling of greater self-worth. Such intangible benefits compensate for the drudgery, monotony and low pay. But it cannot be overlooked that a job outside the home results in less time at home. The children already miss their father; now they will miss their mother, too. This creates feelings of guilt, particularly if the spouse does not provide moral support.

Another dilemma is how to integrate the husband into everyday life. The more the emphasis is placed on his sharing the tasks at home, the greater is the change, both when he comes home and when he leaves. To avoid too great changes, the mother often takes on most of it. In his absence she tries to replace him; the family must function as if it were complete. To make certain that the empty space is not too big when he leaves, the family almost has to function as if he was not present.

A third problem arises in connection with child rearing. In household based fisheries, fishing is a family tradition: son follows father. Therefore, to have the father as a role model is important for recruitment in the fishery, and it is natural to "idolize" him. His absence, however, gives cause to "blame" him. He is not home to participate in family activities. The children thus receive mixed signals. Almost none of the women interviewed in our study wanted their husbands to find another type of work, but few contemplated a son following in his father's footsteps; rather the opposite. The young fellow who wants to be a fisherman must go against his mother's wishes in order to follow his father.

HARDSHIP

When the husband's income fails, then the wife's job becomes the important one. The crisis increases the responsibility. How will she manage her everyday tasks? It will work, because women work until their work is done, even if it interferes with their sleep. Many also develop another way of sharing the housework. It is true, the father is cut off from sharing the general housework when the fishery is on, but during the home period he may dig in fully. He is not someone who is just there on a visit.

It is most important to have a network to rely on. A good neighbour may be a great help, but the best is a nearby grandmother. Grandmother is flexible, she doesn't have fixed opening and closing hours, as do day care centres; she doesn't keep track of time and does not insist on her rights.[1] It is sufficient to show gratitude that she is around. But there is a catch to this: Where are the boundaries? How much and how often can one ask for help? The day care centre, if one is available, may be the answer, because here it clearly defines what one can demand and how the accounts are to be settled.

The importance of family and community contacts illustrates how vulnerable the fishermen's families are in everyday life. They are dependent on support from the immediate environment. The frightening thing about outmigration is not only that there will be fewer inhabitants in the coastal communities, but also that the local informal care system unravels as a result.

THE ROLE OF THE SEXES

It is not possible to create a viable fishing community, even if the resource base is reinstated, unless the families of fishermen and the industry in general function in a manner satisfactory to both husbands and wives. Therefore, fisheries policy must deal with gender equality.

The trend towards more equality between the sexes in society as a whole also applies to the families of fishermen. Our study revealed several lines of development. Figure 3 illustrates this.

Square 1 provides a base to start from: she is involved in his activity as ground crew, while he does not share her territory. From here, three lines go out, which all qualify for the designation "increased equality." Square 2 involves a situation with greater specialization, where she looks after fewer ground crew tasks than she once did, for example, because she is employed outside the home. In square 3, he takes over some of her tasks. Our study found that he generally looked after the children, but did very little housework.

Figure 3

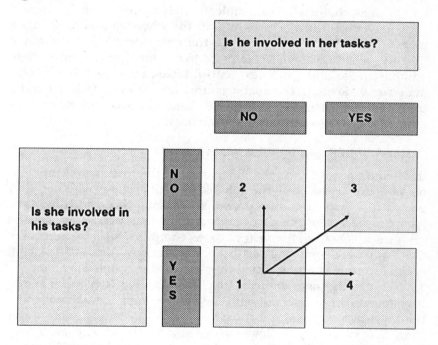

In square 4, they cross each other's boundaries. She finds paid employment, while he takes over the unpaid caring tasks. If this represents the future, then many fishermen's families are already there. Maybe there is a sign in square 4 that it will be more common in the future for women to be aboard fishing vessels? Eva Munk-Madsen (1990) estimated in a study that 2.3 percent of those recorded in Fishermen's Census (Fiskarmanntallet) were women who were actively fishing.

IS THE ROLE OF THE GROUND CREW PASSÉ?

Square 2 has created a hypothesis for a follow-up study of ground crew tasks. The study (Thiessen *et al.* 1991) tried (among other things), to answer the question whether fishermen's wives are about to leave these tasks. First of all, there is no noticeable reduction in answered that they contribute just as much today as five years ago, 38 percent said they contributed less and 21 percent that they do more.

Both husband and wife were asked about which tasks she took care of, which tasks they would want her to carry out, and what they believed the other partner wanted to do. The assumption was that the barriers were in the household itself, in their work preferences and in their abilities to communicate their wishes to each other.

On average, the study found that the wives wanted to be much more involved in ground crew tasks than they were. The men wanted that as well, to an even greater degree. This applied not only to administrative and more sex-neutral tasks, such as filing income tax returns, keeping the boat accounts and dealing with the bank, but also to traditionally, "masculine" tasks, such as repairing equipment and getting spare parts for the boat.

FEMALE FISHER OR FISHERWOMAN?

In our data it was found that 86 percent of the wives were employed outside the home, but the job did not determine whether they contributed less now than previously. Among those with full time jobs, 23 percent of the wives answered that they did more ground crew work now than five years ago, as compared with 20 percent of them who were employed part-time or seasonally. Almost 50 percent of the full-time workers stated they did just as much work now.

Nor did the data indicate that maintaining the ground crew functions is on its way out with the older women. On the contrary, the average age of those women who said they helped more today than five years ago is lower than among those who said they contributed less (36.4 against 41.8 years). It is also worth noting that those women who said they helped more today than five years ago had, on the average, been married/common-law for more than 14 years. That is lower than for those who stated that they do less (slightly over 19 years).

The wife's wish to go in the boat with her husband should be mentioned specifically, because it represents the greatest break with the old sex roles. Nine percent of the wives said they fished with their husbands, while a total of 40 percent would like to do it, if it was up to them. The husband's preference went even further. Forty-four percent of the men would prefer that their wives came along fishing. This is remarkable, particularly when we remember the old taboo against having women on board ships.

When they both want her to come along, what prevents it? Could it be that she thinks he doesn't want her there? Our figures do not support this assumption. Fifty-one percent of the wives believed that their husbands would want them to come along. The reason may be that he does not think she would want to come and therefore does not ask her to. Even this does not explain the low number of women who participate in the fisheries. Forty-one percent of the men believed that wives would like to come along.

What is the problem then? Several explanations are possible. For one thing, household tasks make it difficult to get away. Eva Munk-Madsen found in her study that most of the wives who fish with their husbands are mature in age with most of the childrearing behind them. It may also be that the woman already has another job or that the ground crew tasks are the barrier. Another obstacle could be that she experiences, or expects, disapproval by the local community, based on what is considered appropriate for women. And last but not least, it could be that both husband and wife have at the back of their minds the risk of an accident.

EMPLOYMENT POTENTIAL

It is an important discovery that the ground crew functions are not in the process of being abandoned, or that the women wish they were. We have to assume that when so many women stated that they would like greater involvement, this is because they find the work meaningful and interesting. The fact that the men also have a positive attitude indicates their need for her input.

Thus, the opportunities for increased employment for women in the fishing districts are there. Not only is there an unsatisfied demand for ground crew services, but there is also an unsatisfied willingness to work. The challenge is to find some way of crossing the barriers which prevent willingness (supply) and demand from meeting.

There may be a need for new forms of organization. The household as a vehicle for supplying these services is inadequate. One reason is that the wife's wish to make a greater contribution only meets half of his needs, according to our study. Instead, or preferably in addition to other work, the ground crew functions could be taken over by other enterprises like "line baiting" centres, which were established in many coastal communities at the end of the 1970s. In such plants, the women have not only duties, but rights. In addition, her job would be based on the demands of all the local and visiting fleets and not only on the needs of her husband. This would provide greater job security.

The problem of moving the ground crew tasks from the home to a business is that the labour which is now free would have to be paid; the fisherman would have to pay for a service he previously received for nothing. The present fisheries crisis has removed purchasing power, so the time may not be ripe to establish such enterprises. However, when the situation returns to normal, the reason for doing it will also return. Now is the time to plan how to organize and finance such enterprises.

An important demand on such enterprises would be that their operation be geared to make it possible for the wives to look after responsibilities at home as well, that is, it must be possible to combine ground crew work and caring tasks. The wives of fishermen have a particularly great need for flexibility in their everyday lives. In order for this need to be met, it may be necessary for the women themselves to take the initiative and the control.

A Growth Industry Heading for a Fall?   10

Norwegian fish farming—the raising of salmon in ocean cages—has many noteworthy features. One is the formidable growth which has made it a multi-million dollar industry in the course of a few years. From the early 1970s up to now, production figures have increased by almost 40 percent every year. In 1988, the industry as a whole provided full-time or part-time work for about 7,000 people. (Of these workers, about 30 percent were women.)

Also noteworthy is how the growth has proceeded. Rather than small farms developing into bigger fish farms, the trend has been towards more numerous small scale operations. This was part of a government development strategy to support existing small communities. In 1989, a total of nearly 1,000 fish farms were in operation, of which almost half were purely food fish plants. A study carried out on behalf of the Coastal Expertise Committee, which will be the focus of this chapter, found that 78 percent of the farms employed five people or less and 90 percent employed fewer than 10 people (Holm *et al.* 1990).

A third point is that this growth has benefitted the outlying districts. The peripheral coastal districts have benefitted more from fish farming than have the central ones. More peripheral municipalities are engaged in fish farming and, on average, they have more plants than those in the central fish farming municipalities (Holm *et al.* 1990).

A fourth point is the growth in productivity in the industry: the production per full-time employee rose from 25 metric tonnes in 1985 to 33 metric tonnes in 1988—an increase of 32 percent.

A fifth, and no less startling feature is that the fish farming industry has been very profitable. In 1985, the average total profitability (profit as percent of invested capital) in the fish hatchery sector was 30 percent, while the corresponding figure for food fish was 18.5 percent. This is high compared to other branches of industry. Admittedly, the drop in market price has weakened profitability in recent years, but a bright future for the industry is still predicted in the long run.

CURIOUSER AND CURIOUSER

Individually, these are surprising features; most remarkable, however, is that they manifested themselves at the same time. It seems quite curious that the country's foremost growth industry was developed in the periphery, based on local initiative and by businesses organized as family enterprises. The question is therefore unavoidable—what is the explanation?

It is common to point to Norway's favourable natural conditions for fish farming. We have the advantage of a long coastline protected by islands and shoals. The environment is clean and the Gulf Stream provides mild sea temperatures favourable to the growth of fish. Market opportunities have also been good, even if it has required a lot of effort to develop them. Countries such as Denmark, France and, until recently, the U.S.A. have been our most important markets. It has been possible to find new markets all the time.

The fact that our coastline is inhabited has been important. Where the natural conditions for fish farming were good, there were also active local communities. The significance of this can be seen when we compare it with, for example, the west coast of Canada, where fish farming has been built up in uninhabited areas. There, in addition to establishing the fish farms, they have had to create support structures, housing, roads, electrical power and other facilities. Their investment in establishing fish farming has therefore been much higher than ours.

In Norway, fish farmers had only to "plug in" to the existing physical and social infrastructure. Fish farming could also benefit from the traditional fishing industry. Feed made from fish was readily available from the processing industry and a wealth of knowledge about how to treat and market fish was there for the asking. The various institutions of the fishing industry were also applicable to the fish farming industry (the Raw Fish Act being a good example).

These are, nevertheless, only the basic conditions for starting fish framing; they have meant a lot, but not everything. It remains to explain how these conditions have been effectively utilized. Behind this formidable growth are investments by a large number of people, from north to south, rich in initiative and willing to take risks.

The licensing system has contributed to the characteristically small-scale farms by preventing enterprises from expanding. It also contributed to the expansion being scattered along the coast (thereby benefitting the outlying areas). The licensing system alone, however, does not explain why we have so many fish farmers. It has only prevented the number from increasing.

FISH FARMING ENVIRONMENT

It is important to emphasize the significance of the effect of the social environment. Today there are fish farms in almost 44 percent of the municipalities in the country—a wide geographic spread. Our study found, though, that 8 percent of the municipalities held half of the food fish licences. In other words, the industry has been developed, to a great degree, in certain geographically concentrated environments. The Norwegian fish farming industry appears to be both scattered and concentrated at the same time. This is interesting because it can only be partially explained by government control through the licensing system. Many of these clusters were well established when the licensing regulations became a real barrier to starting new farms at the end of the 1970s.

Fish farming started at a time when knowledge of the biological and marketing conditions was limited and relatively untested. The development was not under the aegis of established industrial businesses with strong financial backing, private research expertise and well-established sales channels. The pioneers were enterprising individuals, who ventured into the unknown and, hungering for knowledge, learned by trial and error—their own and that of others.

The fish farming industry illustrates the importance of industrial networking dealt with in Chapter 5. The growth in the fish farming industry can be explained as the result of a social process in which fish farmers exchange knowledge and become role models for newcomers. By demonstrating that it is possible, and by personally exchanging advice and experience, pioneers inspire others in the area to begin fish farming. The network functions both as an information exchange and a teaching institution. When the farmers meet, friendly chatter soon becomes technical discussion—and then it doesn't take long before somebody reaches the conclusions that, "If he can do it, I can do it, too."

BLOTTING PAPER

The absence of competition on a local level eases communication between the farmers. They have no interest in hiding information from each other, as fishermen may have when they are out on the grounds. The competition "would only be to be the very best," said one farmer in an interview. It is no disadvantage to those who have established themselves that new people are starting up. On the contrary, it creates an environment where everybody has a chance to become even better.[1]

Due to such learning environments, the growth curve becomes progressive. A new farmer provides the basis for establishing many new relationships between farmers locally and in the outside world. The network is constantly being expanded and deepened. Little by little, this develops into a basis for cooperation and common investment.

Geographic distances limit the social network somewhat. As well, we are running out of areas in which to farm. The natural and social conditions for fish farming are not equally good everywhere. The growth may be compared to when ink is dropped on blotting paper—the spot expands somewhat and then stops.

In some cases, private initiative has started the process of setting up a farm. In others, it is the municipal authorities who have been involved. An example of the latter is Herøy municipality in Nordland province, where the municipality some time ago created their own co-operative to help the farmers get started. The co-op provided them with advice and guidelines as well as material such as smolt and feed. The co-op also provided operating credit, insurance, veterinary services, and it looked after slaughtering, packaging, marketing and sales.

A SATURATED MARKET

Such local, spontaneous processes, with or without district/municipal participation, created the fish farming industry which is today an international giant. This weakens the claim that lack of entrepreneurship is the problem in the coastal districts. It is rather the opposite: the will to start fish farming has, at times, far exceeded the licenses available and has turned licensing documents into securities.

The problem with such spontaneous growth processes is that they often run amok; the expansion is too fast. If the demand increases through old markets expanding and new markets being developed, the supply increases still faster because of these positive signals received from the market. The result is inevitable—the market becomes saturated, and prices drop. Many farms have experienced problems and bankruptcies have been unavoidable. It has in this way reinforced the coastal crisis. The fish farming industry has not functioned as the buffer it could have been.

The tragedy of the commons which the fishermen are experiencing on the water is being experienced by the fish farmers in the market as well. It might have been avoided if the industry had consisted of fewer and larger units. Control would have been simpler and there would have been fewer investment decisions to monitor. Rationalization of the structure is likely to be the result of the financial problems being experienced by many fish farms today. The regional consequences of such a development will, however, be negative. It is therefore well worthwhile to look for other ways of attacking the problem.

Some possibilities may be found in better organization and management. Here the challenges are great and complicated, but not insoluble. The industry's own organizations have taken the initiative. It is interesting to note that the Fish Farmers' Sales Association (Fiskeoppdretternes Salgslag) has intervened to regulate the market by organizing freezing of surplus fish. Regulation of supply could, of course, be defined as a responsibility of the government, as it is in the fisheries.

The basic conditions for individual fish farmers have been significantly altered by the market inhibiting growth. From now on it will be important to operate a farm as cost-effectively as possible. The key will be operator expertise: the efficiency of the operation will depend, to a great degree, on what the operator knows and learns. Expertise will become as important a production factor as water lots, technology and capital.

The fish farmers handle a live product. This represents a challenge which the managers of fish processing plants are spared. To operate a fish farm therefore requires considerable all-round knowledge. One must have some knowledge—not necessarily in-depth knowledge—in many fields, such as finance, administration, production and information technology, biology and disease.

WHO IS A FISH FARMER?

What about the level of competence in the fish farming industry? How high is it? What is being done to increase it? These were some of the questions posed in a study for the Coastal Expertise Committee. Few fish farmers have "grown up with" the industry, as has been the pattern in the open-water fishing industry. That is only to be expected in an industry barely 20 years old. The fish farmers got their trades training in other industries and types of work.

A large proportion of the fish farmers do have backgrounds in the fishing industry. Twenty-three percent were previously fishermen, and slightly less than 4 percent were in fish processing. This is of course no accident. The knowledge they acquired as fishermen or fish processors is of great value in fish farming. Even for animal farmers, the leap into fish farming is not so great. Our study found that 10 percent of the fish farmers were, or still are, animal farmers.

That fish farming is attractive to animal farmers and fishermen is not only because they have appropriate qualifications, but also because they can still continue to operate and live in the same way as before. Fish farming can be operated as a small family enterprise in which one can be self-employed. About half of all fish farming operations are family businesses and most are established in the harbour at home. Fish farming can often be combined with other activities and one out of three farmers has another occupation.

Nevertheless, in the first years of fish farming, when licensing was just a formality, opportunities were open to anyone. The result is an industry operated by people with a variety of backgrounds. We recorded a total of 80 different occupations represented, including pilots, oil workers, veterinarians, truck owners, dental assistants, linemen, sales consultants, equipment contractors, pharmaceutical technicians and divers. Only 10 percent had been in the fish farming industry before. It is also worth mentioning that three out of four had no management experience before they ventured into fish farming.

It is only in recent years that technical qualifications have been required in order to be granted a licence. Today, such requirements can be met because education in fish farming has been much improved, both at the secondary and higher levels. More than 20 percent of Norwegian fish farmers have secondary education in aquaculture, a corresponding proportion has higher education and only 20 percent is without any type of advanced education. In contrast, the study of North Norwegian managers of fish processing plants (referred to in previous chapters) found that 60 percent had no advanced education. In other words, fish farmers are considerably better prepared educationally than their colleagues in the fish processing industry.

WILLINGNESS TO LEARN

There is a high level of willingness to learn in the fish farming industry. Eight out of ten fish farmers stated that they participated in post-educational courses in the two years preceding our study. Just as many have visited exhibitions and read trade magazines regularly. This is double the number we found when the same questions were asked of managers of fish processing plants.

The study found other indications of willingness to learn. First of all, cooperation between fish farmers was widespread. Secondly, one out of three farmers is on the board of another fish farming operation. Both types of contact promote learning. It is also common to recruit people to one's own board to acquire added expertise; half of the people affirmed that they have outsiders on the board who provide the operation with extra expertise. Thirdly, expertise can be increased by acquiring well-trained workers. More than 50 percent of fish farmers employed people with secondary or higher education in mariculture.

An interesting finding of the study was that the higher the educational background of the fish farmers, the more extroverted were their style of managing the operation. They travelled more, were on many boards or committees; they read several trade magazines, cooperated more with other fish farmers and invested in recruiting employees with high expertise. In other words, there is a connection between the expertise of the operators, their management style and the recruitment of workers. It is therefore no surprise that well educated fish farmers are also involved in FOU activities to a great extent: one out of four, according to our survey.

Tracing the effects of an extroverted management style on increased profitability is another matter. It is difficult to measure such effects because, among other things, they are long-term, and it is hard to attach a realistic value to time. It is expensive to be constantly travelling. Daily contact with what is happening at home is lost. Profitability is secured not only on far-away ice, but also on home ice. Our study found that any extroverted activity is not in addition to, but instead of, introverted activity.

NEW CHALLENGES

Present-day fish farmers are in a different situation from those who started up first. The pioneers had to break new ground, the knowledge base was skimpy and the technology uncertain. There were no cages, dry feed was unknown and special packaging had not been developed. No organization was in place and the authorities were not really interested in fish farming. The pioneers had to experiment and trust their own strength (Didriksen 1990).

Those who started up later have been able to get support from established institutions. They have been able to draw on well-tested technology which they, unlike the pioneers, can buy on the market. Today, fish farming uses cages in which the fish are automatically fed with dry feed. The product is shipped in special packaging in refrigerated trucks and airplanes to markets near and far. Just about all Norwegian fish farmers are members of a technical and a financial organization which handles contacts with government departments and markets. Mariculture has now become a national priority field of research.

All this makes life somewhat easier for the fish farmers in that conditions for operating scattered and small-scale farms have improved. But the farmers still meet challenges which the pioneers did not have to worry about. Diseases and other environmental problems have become new threats. As soon as research finds remedies for some diseases, new ones surface. In addition, new environmental requirements are introduced that depend on technology that has not yet been developed.

Moving farming installations on to land, or the use of other "closed" systems to prevent contagion, is not very popular—less than 10 percent of the farmers use such methods. This technology is considerably more capital-intensive than the traditional cages in the ocean.

Cage technology has made fish farming possible in small units. If land-based installations succeed, the question will be whether it is still possible to maintain the small-scale structures. Moreover, our natural conditions for fish farming will no longer be a comparative advantage. But we do have a head start, thanks to the expertise in fish farming we have developed and to the markets cultivated over the years.

CONTINUED GROWTH?

Developments in the fish farming industry have, until now, proceeded by leaps and bounds, and there is little to indicate that it will soon flatten out. According to a "A Perspective Sketch of Norwegian Mari-Culture" ("Perspektivskisse for norsk havbruk") prepared by The National (Norwegian) Committee for Ocean Farming Research, (Det Nasjonale Utvalg for Havbruksforskning) the present growth is merely an overture. The Committee estimates that by the year 2,000 the production of farmed fish in Norway will be about 400–500,000 metric tonnes as opposed to 150,000 metric tonnes in 1990. This projection, however, presupposes a breakthrough in sea ranching and the raising of species other than salmon.

If the development proceeds as expected, then there will be a multifold increase in production within this decade. The committee feels that there are good prospects of Norway becoming a world leader in the supply of seafood. A great potential is envisaged through combining the traditional fishery with ocean farming. For example, methods of strengthening weak year classes of wild fish through cultivation are under discussion.

What the actual results of such developments would mean for the coastal districts is not easy to predict. Already today, the fish farming industry has environmental and marketing problems which would be compounded by the quantities of fish now envisaged. It is not just a matter of producing half a million tonnes of fish, but of finding markets at remunerative prices. In addition, area conflicts could be intensified. Extensive sea ranching could raise new regulation problems. How to divide the rights to fish these species could become a Gordian knot.

Despite these clouds on the horizon, it is difficult to avoid catching the optimism of leading researchers in ocean farming. Not all contagion in the fish farming industry is harmful! If things work out as the researchers believe, then the economy and the population along the coast will have a far more secure foundation than today.

VALUABLE LOCAL COMMUNITIES

The history of Norwegian fish farming should have taught us one thing: there are great values in local coastal communities. One is the infrastructure, another is the knowledge and traditions perpetuated by the people. Without these, Norwegian fish farming would not have been the success it is today. There is a constant challenge to find new uses for these resources.

The fish farming industry also shows the significance of indigenous development of the economy of the coastal communities. The industry grew out of the coastal communities themselves; it was not transplanted there from the outside. That is evident from the ownership structure. In 1989, almost 70 percent of the fish farming businesses were locally owned in full. In almost 83 percent, the local ownership share was more than 50 percent.

The licensing system contributed to securing ties to the local community. At times it was probably a hindrance to the supply of capital and, for that reason, the authorities elected to relax the conditions. This local control has, however, helped to prevent conflicts which could easily have occurred between the old and new fishing industries. Fish farming has slipped into what Ståle Seierstad (1985) calls "the coastal occupational field" without any problems. Instead of creating competition between the old coastal occupations and the new, they have complemented each other.

Again, comparisons can be drawn with other countries which have tried fish farming. In Canada and the U.S.A., the fishermen are often strong opponents of fish farming; local roots are feeble and fish farming has far weaker organizational ties to the traditional fisheries sector.

Like the fish processing industry, the fish farming industry is faced with the challenge of ensuring local ties in the years to come. The licensing system is a necessary, but not necessarily a sufficient, means. The National (Norwegian) Committee for Ocean Farming Research recognizes the need to create greater integration between fish farmers in ways which at the same time ensure individual autonomy and small-scale operation. There is also great potential for strengthening ties between fish farming and the fishing industry in general. This may be the solution to the problem of endangered local connections. But such arrangements will not likely come about by themselves. It is clearly a task for organizations within both industries, as well as for the municipalities in their planning and work projects.

A Market for Tradition?   11

The livelihood of the fishing population has both an economic and a cultural base. While the economic foundation is related to natural resources and international markets, the cultural base is connected to experience and tradition in the local community. The problem for coastal Norway is that there may be a conflict between them. There is a challenge to become market-oriented without casting traditions aside—to convert what one has and what one can do into something others need and want, without "emptying the barrel."

OLD-FASHIONED COASTAL CULTURE?

The coastal crisis has caused many people to feel that there is no value in tradition, either materially or culturally. They feel that tradition is synonymous with "old-fashioned," that it is a hindrance to development, and that the conclusion is obvious: to succeed in the markets, tradition must be sacrificed.

Such a conclusion is not particularly conducive to creating optimism and the courage to forge ahead. Rather, the result will be uncertainty and anxiety about the future of life along the coast. The crisis is not the only thing creating pessimism—its solutions also give rise to concern.

Ask any fisherman's family what they want their children to become and they are clear one point: they don't want them to become fishermen, and certainly not fish plant workers. The parents are well aware of the dilemma: the home district depends on someone carrying on those vocations. They feel nevertheless, their children should not take a chance on anything the local community has to offer. When Gunda Nilsen, a fisherman's wife in Nordland, asked Fisheries Minister Svein Munkejord for advice about what she should tell her children, now that the crisis has paralyzed the coast, she received no useful reply.[1]

It is not so easy to see what we have—and may lose—if traditions are condemned. Culture is invisible for those who share it; it is taken for granted. In this respect, the crisis appears to have had a positive effect. It has made it clear that it is not only important to safeguard livelihoods, but also the way of life along the coast. Those who have followed the Norwegian fisheries policy debate know that it has been many years since the problem has been defined in this way. We probably have to go back to the dispute about the seines in the Lofoten fishery in the 1950s to find such arguments.

COASTAL CULTURE AS A SALES PRODUCT

The coastal culture can be used for more than producing fish. It has a market value in itself. It is not only the Saami who are now on display as a tourist commodity. The coastal communities also have special characteristics which tourists are willing to pay to experience. For example, a report to the Provincial Legislature in Nordland concerning tourism states:

> The fishing stations with their shanties as characteristic features continue to be the leading symbol with great and increasing attraction for tourists.

The travel industry promises a bright future for coastal communities and is put forward in the provincial plans as a new field of endeavour. It promises to create some desperately needed jobs for women. Provincial plans provide funding for making the coastal communities more accessible and inviting. Lofoten, perhaps our most distinctive fishing area, is singled out as "an international attraction" and the coastal fleet as "a tourism resource." According to *Fiskeribladet* (4 October 1990), Nord Trøndelag province is thinking along the same lines.

Local and regional authorities are not alone in seeing great potential in the tourism industry. The National (Norwegian) Committee for Ocean Farming Research is also of the opinion that there are great opportunities for tourism. The Committee believes, for example, that the fish farming industry could form the basis for establishing "marine parks."

The basis for the belief in tourism as a new coastal industry is, among other things, that it has properties which the fishing industry is lacking. A draft tourism plan for Lofoten states:

> The tourism industry is a service industry and is special, because, among other things, the distribution and consumption take place

by the customers being brought to the product and not the reverse, as is the case with industries that produce commodities.

The export of a tonne of salt fish creates a ripple effect in the local community, but it is limited to the needs and demands of the employees in the fishing and transportation industries, etc. The customer—the consumer of the fish—does not cause any further ripple effects once the fish has been shipped abroad.

Thus, there are good reasons to have high hopes for the tourism industry. The coast has much to offer and the demand is growing.

IDENTITY IN DANGER?

Even though there is a great potential in the tourism industry, opinions are sharply divided. Many feel that it would ruin the special cultural characteristics; that the authenticity would be lost. It is even claimed that the tourism industry would reduce the coastal culture to a caricature of itself. There is a danger of devaluation through commercialization. The value of culture is, in one sense, reduced the moment a price is set on it. When hospitality becomes a business it becomes less genuine and honest, as those who have travelled in Southern Europe can attest. Both buyer and seller feel a degradation of value the moment culture is made the object of business transactions.

In the provincial plan for Nordland (1988–91), it is suggested that "special local cultural traditions and values are in the process of losing out to values which are created nationally and internationally"; it is therefore "a challenge to enhance the special local tradition of values and culture which contribute to creating a feeling of identity with and belonging to a local community, a region or a province." Any investment in tourism would make this task more difficult, particularly if marketing follows the textbooks and emphasizes "market orientation" instead of "product orientation." The first is based on what the tourists ask for; the second, on what one has to offer.

What the tourists ask for is not necessarily an unrefined product (Kamfjord 1990). Product development is needed. The special cultural features must be smoothed off and polished to function as a saleable product. The risk is that not only could the coastal culture be changed, but that it could be transformed into something else. Instead of growth, we get outgrowths. This danger is present particularly if the development of the tourism product occurs without local participation and control.

MANNA FROM HEAVEN?

But the future need not be so bleak. It is not clear that encounters between coastal populations and international mass tourism will result in the ruin of their cultural identity. Maybe the opposite will happen. As pointed out by the British anthropologist Anthony Cohen (1985), it is often in meeting with the unknown that we understand ourselves. Others are the mirrors in which we recognize ourselves.

Marketing the coastal culture as a product for tourism presumes conscious awareness of the area's special qualities. Much good can come from such a process. It may strengthen rather than weaken local identity. Some people say that tourism does not undermine local culture, but instead provides it with an extra leg to stand on. There are even those who maintain that tourism is manna from heaven, the salvation of a culture which would otherwise be lost. Ever since the shanties in Lofoten have been rented out to tourists outside the fishing season it has been easier to maintain them. This has benefitted the tourists and the local population, as well as the visiting fishermen during the Lofoten fishing season.

The Coastal Expertise Committee also hopes that the travel industry will contribute to strengthening the fishing industry. "Any organization of tourism facilities in connection with the fishing industry could contribute to increased knowledge and understanding by other parts of the population of the way in which the industry exploits the production potential of the ocean" (The Coastal Expertise Committee Action plan 1990, p. 8).

The tourism industry is not likely to represent salvation "come Hell or high water." Much depends on how the meeting between tourists and the local population is organized. Packaged tours reduce the tourist to a passive observer and the local inhabitant to a photo object. Instead of mutual learning, the old stereotypes about what "they" are like are easily reinforced. Therefore, a real interaction between the two parties must be organized, through which they may learn from one another. The tourist must be allowed to become a participant, not just a spectator.

ULTIMA THULE: "THE END OF THE WORLD"

Whether the special cultural characteristics will be threatened depends on how investments are made. It is important to ensure that "what is genuine and unfalsified in the everyday life of coastal Norway"—to quote the tourism plan for Vesterålen region—remain genuine and unfalsified after the development has taken place. In this the tourists and the local inhabitants truly have common interests. The Americans may be brought up on hamburgers and French fries, but they, more so than we, would find a MacDonald's out of place in Henningsvær.

Beautiful, natural and exotic environments must be designated and identified before they become tourist attractions. This in itself, however, is not sufficient. Trollfjorden makes a mighty impression, but Johan Boyer's dramatic story of the Trollfjord battle in the novel *The Last Viking* increases the fascination. From one perspective, the North Cape plateau is only a bare cliff. The appeal increases when it is marketed as "the end of the world"—Ultima Thule. It also helps that a stone has been raised in memory of King Oscar II's visit after his coronation in 1873, as has been done at another tourist attraction, Saltstraumen, which he visited on his voyage north.

Such markers help imbue the attraction with a mythical aura. It makes the experience more memorable and it simplifies marketing. But if the intention of the new tourist centre on the North Cape plateau was to add to the designation of the cliff as a mythical travel goal, then it has failed—in fact, the centre has spoilt it. Ann Helene Arntzen (1989) states that "the cliff in its mythical sense is gone," and a study by Arvid Viken (1989) of Finnmark District College found that half of the visitors felt the tourist centre diminished the experience. It may seem like an understatement when a tourist brochure about the coastal ferry *Hurtigruta* says:

> In the new North Cape centre you can eat and drink well and buy souvenirs as a reminder of the site where Europe comes to a sudden full stop against the North. But for most people, the experience of an endless view northward towards nothing is probably stronger than the pleasure of knowing that the services of civilisation have arrived here as well.

FROM COMMONS TO COLONY?

The paradox is that such designations may easily become the main attraction. They may even become conditions for investment. The demand for return on investment could therefore supplant considerations for the preservation of an authentic experience.

The developments which have taken place at North Cape illustrate another problem, familiar from the fishing industry: the tendency to privatize the commons. The most controversial aspect of the whole North Cape project, according to newspaper debates, is that a fee is now demanded to be allowed out onto the plateau itself. The fee—the "resource rent"—benefits the developer, not the public or the local inhabitants.

This may be only the beginning, since each tourist product is related to development costs which must be met, preferably from sources other than the public purse. If privatization of the commons is to be the pattern for the travel industry in coastal regions, then we may expect conflicts similar to those we have experienced in connection with the fishing regulations. The headline in *Nordlys*— "To arms against SAS (Scandinavian Airlines System) fees on North Cape" (12 February 1991)—looked much like those about fisheries regulations.

Researchers who have studied the social consequences of the tourist industry internationally are looking at the question of who wins and who loses. Some claim that tourism has become a new form for imperialism. The investors are international concerns, the profit is taken out of the area and the local population is left behind, picked clean. This may also soon become a problem in Norway. There is an obvious risk in putting aside the interests of the local population. They have no "deed" to their own culture. They are not protected in the same way as the real property rights to fishing vessels.

PARASITES

The travel industry in itself has little to offer beyond easy transportation and comfortable hotel beds. In this sense, it is a "parasite" on traditional industries, on local culture and nature. When SAS advertises "travel experiences," we must assume that it is not the air travel which represents the experience, but the destination. Admittedly, the tourist needs room and board during the stay, which may be a basis for some profitable investments, but the hotel bed is only the means and not the destination.

It is only the coastal ferry which is a " product of experience" in itself. It is a sailing community or a "settlement in motion," as Erling Welle Strand called it in 1953 (Jacobsen 1989). That it brings the tourists through beautiful scenery is, of course, important. But the trip along the coast from Bergen to Kirkenes is even more saleable because the ferry calls in at active local communities, where people are doing things other than preening in front of the tourists.

It is no longer taken for granted that local communities must be active to function as tourist products. To reduce overproduction of agricultural products within the EC (European Community), support is now given to converting farms into combined guest homes and zoological gardens for city dwellers. Should we copy this to reduce the overcapacity in the fishing industry? Closed fishing stations could become fish restaurants (this is already being tried in Henningsvær), or hotels, as in Mefjordvær. Fishing vessels without quotas could be used for mini-cruises or whale watching, as in Vesterålen. Or, tourists could be given a chance to be "a fisherman for a day," as in Moskenes.

The thought might cross one's mind that this could be a safety net for the coastal culture in times of crisis. But this is not well founded. When a fishing community or station is reduced to a backdrop for the travel industry, it loses its attraction value. And it will also no longer be attractive as a place to live.

Thus, fishing policy also becomes tourism policy. Regulations which emphasize centralization—which undermine the inshore fisheries and could result in fishing stations being closed down and which, again, could result in the young people seeing no future in the fishing industry—would, in the end, also affect the travel industry. A new coastal industry cannot be exchanged for the old. Fish cannot be exchanged for tourists. It is, rather, that the new industry requires the old. If tourism is entered into with common sense and understanding, then the old industry might even gain from the new.

MASS TOURISM

The travel industry is growing rapidly internationally and is expected to become the world's largest industry by the year 2000. Up to now, Norway has not managed to exploit this market very much. Instead, we have lost market share. Norwegians spend more money on vacations abroad than foreigners do in Norway. It is therefore not unreasonable for the authorities and the industry to see possibilities opening up. The untouched nature and the deep-rooted culture that the coast can offer is viewed as a resource. And when the coast is in financial difficulty, the conclusion is obvious—we must gamble on tourism.

However, the paradox is that once the pristine nature and unfalsified culture are exploited for tourist purposes, they easily lose their value. As an English saying goes: "You can't have your cake and eat it too." Studies have found that precisely this lack of mass tourism is an important reason for tourists selecting Norway as their destination (Brinchmann and Jensen 1990; Jervan et al. 1986). Coastal Norway cannot be marketed as an area without mass tourism and at the same time appeal to it. Even if it does succeed, it won't work in the long run.

What is needed is a clear and conscious decision about which segments of the market one wants to appeal to. It is possible to avoid mass tourism if plans are properly laid. Small-scale communities require small-scale tourism. Now, the key words are so-called "eco-tourism," "green tourism," or "soft tourism." It is along these lines that tourism plans are being developed for Lofoten and Vesterålen regions. Lofoten, for example, is described as follows:

> The development of the travel industry in Lofoten must primarily be to nurture and strengthen the present traditions and special characteristics of the region to the benefit of both the local population and the tourists. It is the special characteristics that the tourists want to experience and which draw them here ... We must guard against Lofoten being developed into an impersonal tourist machine ... (we must) regulate the flow of tourists so that Lofoten will remain a vacation goal without mass tourism also in the future.

A GLOBAL TRAVEL INDUSTRY PRODUCT

Both the fishing industry and the travel industry tax the resources of the commons, and in both industries there is a risk of ruining the basis of their existence. And is the solution to "the tragedy of the commons" the same for both industries?

Both industries lend themselves to bureaucratic manipulation, where the local level is at the end of a long chain of control with a central starting point. As in the fishing industry, there is a possibility that local interests will be run over roughshod. Liberalization and privatization are no guarantee against it happening, in either the one or the other industry. On the contrary, the chances of this happening are increased.

Local initiatives need coordination, or the same thing will be offered repeatedly and too much of the same thing will be done. There are areas within the travel sector where the capacity is under-utilized. Not all locations can be called the "gateway" to an area. As well, too many tourist magnets are not good—they neutralize each other.

There is a need for inter-municipal cooperation in order to come up with a common strategy. It is also important to establish a reasonable division of responsibility between the local and the central levels, between the authorities and the industry. Organization is required, just as it is in the fishing industry, where the goal is to create coordination and contact between different administrative levels and those who work in the industry in the region.

The regional travel committees are examples of agencies which establish meeting points between the authorities and the industry. The impression is that, to some degree, they create connections between the travel and fishing industries. But they were certainly not set up with that in mind.

The goal of creating "global travel products," as it is expressed in the tourism plans, will require agencies which have the ability to think globally. Such organizations would benefit both the travel industry and the fishing industry, if tourism is to contribute to the "sustainable development" of the coast.

Crisis

Photographs: Bjørn Tore Forberg (taken when he was a
journalist with the newspaper *Fiskeribladet*).

17 April 1989: the day before the coastal fishery was closed unexpectedly.

18 April 1989: fishery closed.

January 1990: crisis meeting.

May 1987: a Russian and a Norwegian trawler off Bear Island.

Russian trawlers have become part of the town scene in fishing communities (left: a Norwegian vessel).

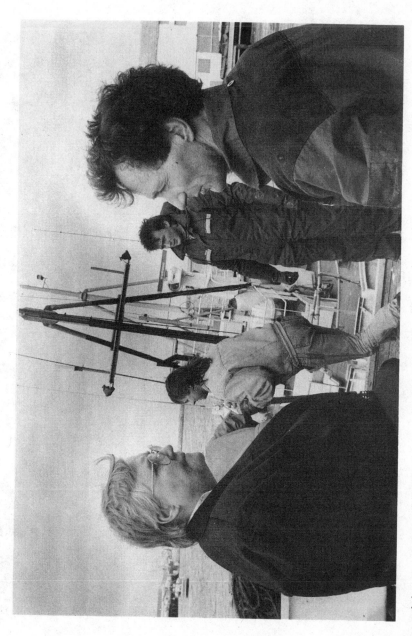

Fisheries minister and fisherman talking cod quotas.

February 1992: the capelin are back: Norwegian purse seiners outside the Russian 12-mile limit.

Packing valuable consumer capelin for Japan.

A Matter of Knowledge? **12**

The fishing industry fluctuates rapidly. Four or five years ago, optimism was high. The fish stocks were in good shape, market prospects were promising and the fishing industry was described as "the opportunities industry." Adam did not dwell long in Paradise; the optimism was short-lived. In 1990 we are back to where we were, except that this time the crisis is worse than ever. Now, it is not only the traditional fishing industry which has problems; the fish farming industry is also hard hit, due to over production and low prices.

How could it have happened? How is it possible to get into such a mess? The slump in prices for farmed salmon should have been avoidable since Norway controls such a large portion of the market. With the 200 mile zone it is not so easy to blame others when important fish stocks collapse. What many in 1972 feared would happen if we became members of the EC (European Community), we have managed to do on our own.

Since the Coastal Expertise Committee has recommended a very strong emphasis on increasing expertise, it is natural to ask if we could have avoided our present difficulties if the level of expertise had been higher. Would it have made any difference, one way or the other?

INDUSTRIAL EXPERTISE

Both the resource crisis and the market crisis are expressions of a systems failure, not the failure of individuals. Both crises stem from to a lack of ability to direct and organize the whole industry. The responsibility rests, first and foremost, with the authorities and industrial organizations, not with individual industrial players.

Therefore, increased expertise among industrial employees will not necessarily solve the problem.

Measures to correct the systems failure do presume accessible expertise, and require an understanding of how intervention in the operation of the industry will affect individuals, groups and regions. This, again, presumes an in-depth knowledge of how the fishing industry functions in one thing or another, big or small. The question is whether the authorities and the industrial organizations have the knowledge required.

In May, 1990, the Regional Committee (Landsdelsutvalget) for North Norway and Namdalen gathered a number of social scientists at a seminar in Tromsø to discuss fisheries regulations. One of the speakers, Bjørn Hersoug from Norwegian College of Fishery Science (Norges Fiskerihøgskole), gave the following description of the regulations:

- Regulations cut the heads off the best. The young fishermen with modern medium-sized boats get the worst of it.
- Regulations have resulted in "Skipper fisheries."[1] Since it is only the boats and boat owners who get quotas, the crews are squeezed out.
- An overreaction has taken place with regard to the smallest boats, which means little in terms of fish quantity, but more in terms of community viability.

A competent management system must be capable of learning from such experiences and correcting the bias. But competent management should also be able to predict such effects, since the damage may prove to be irreparable.

When the Coastal Expertise Committee launches concepts such as "industrial management" and "industrial expertise" as opposed to "unit management" and "unit expertise," then they are, of course, touching on a central point. Not only must development of management and expertise take place in the plants, at sea and on land but also in the administrative and industrial organizations.

LOM (LEADERSHIP, ORGANIZATION AND MANAGEMENT)

In order to be able to increase expertise on an industrial level, the Coastal Expertise Committee suggests investing in LOM-related research into the fishing industry, that is, research into leadership, organization and management. In Norway, LOM is one of the fields of research given national focus, on a par with mariculture and biotechnology. Therefore, the Coastal Expertise Committee's suggestion on this point should definitely be followed up.

First and foremost, we need to study the knowledge base employed in the fisheries policy (MacInnes *et al.* 1991). We need to determine the type of experiences, theories and assumptions that form the basis for management of the fish resources, which learning processes will result in decisions, as well as the system established for the collection of information. We need to know more about the interaction between management and research and the status of the research results in the decision-making process, as well as what is needed to provide for a breakthrough to new knowledge. It would also be interesting to look at the degree to which learning from experience occurs and what conditions hinder or promote such learning.

Knut Dahl Jacobsen's (1965) classic article on fisheries management could be a guide. Is information collected by management itself or is it only made available to them by some interest groups? What role do the professions and interest organizations play in the process? Does bias in participation produce bias in the supply of information, thus resulting in clients being treated differently by management?

MASTERING THE CRISIS

The crisis must be tackled not only on an industry level, but also on a business level. Increased expertise may not have averted the crisis, but might have helped in its handling. It seems reasonable to assume that firms which have invested in expertise will ride out the storm better than those which have not. Well-qualified firms should be better prepared for changes in times of crisis than the others.

The three studies carried out under the auspices of the Coastal Expertise Committee were started before the present crisis came about. Nevertheless, they provide a basis for determining that education and expertise influence how a firm is directed and what it invests in. There are no studies, however, which provide unambiguous answers to whether increased expertise increases the ability to survive a crisis.

Our study interviewed a number of fish farmers in their home communities. One was in a critical situation because of the low prices. He felt that his many outside contacts, which he had acquired throughout the years, were now his most important resource. These contacts give him many opportunities to test ideas and he always has someone to ask for advice, he said. It appears that there is a thread running from high expertise, through an extroverted leadership style to the mastering of a crisis.

MANAGEMENT OF CHANGE

Increased expertise is sensible in both good and bad times, and is a part of what we conceive as "management of change" in the Coastal Expertise Committee's reports. Ups and downs are challenges which require changes in the individual firms. It presumes managers who are not only capable of changing their leadership style, but who can manage their firms to be ready for change. The latter means creating organizations which can learn, both from their own and others' experience, and which can put this knowledge into practice.

There are good reasons for maintaining that small firms, with their simple technology and small bureaucratic form of organization, can reorganize more easily than large firms. But small firms do not necessarily have better opportunities to learn. For one thing, the manager needs time to go back to school. And if anything is lacking in small firms, it is precisely time. The study of North Norwegian fish processing plant managers found that more than half of them had a work week of 60 hours or more, and 20 percent worked more than 70 hours a week. A manager of a small firm is often alone in management. He does not have many chances to leave the operation and, for that reason, does not receive the same stimulation from the outside that an extroverted management style is open to.

A fish farm manager has a less inhuman situation. Even in the busiest summer season he does not work more than an average of 50 hours a week. During the winter season when things are less hectic, his work week is similar to that of a normal wage earner. This helps to make fish farming an attractive industry. It may also function as a fall-back position for burnt-out fishermen and fish-plant managers in many districts. The problem for a fish farmer is, however, that he must be on hand at all times. The fish must be fed and it is difficult to take time off. In this respect, it is like being an agricultural farmer.

We have to conclude that the conditions for increased expertise are not the best for managers in the fish processing industry, although they place considerable emphasis on improving their qualifications. The pressing daily tasks have a tendency to displace long-term and extroverted management tasks. Nor is the prospect optimistic for fishermen. In a study for the Coastal Expertise Committee, Ivar Sagen says that very few of the fishermen see any value in increasing expertise (Sagen maintains that this, in itself, is an expression of low expertise).

META-LEARNING

Network-building as a strategy to increase expertise also interests the Coastal Expertise Committee. There is a widespread notion that the fishing industry consists of individualists who are not capable of cooperating. If that were true, then the prospects for increased expertise through network-building would be poor. This opinion, however, has been exposed as a myth. Two out of three firms already cooperate with other firms, most of it done locally. As well, they are not afraid of conflict areas, such as raw material supplies. (Cooperation in raw material is actually nourished by competition.)

In his study, Ivar Sagen found that fishing boat owners cooperate across a broad spectrum—in, for example, purchases, recruitment of crews, accounting and operational planning. Competition at sea does not prevent cooperation on land. Sagen argues for the importance of establishing new organizational forms in the harvesting link, which would lend themselves to the fishermen jointly being able to realize projects, recruit expertise, make replacement arrangements, and so on.

Our study found that fish farmers also cooperate with each other. In many places, so-called "fish farmer circles" have been developed to enhance fellowship and improve the learning environment on a local level. It is also common for farmers at one plant to hold positions on boards of other fish farming plants, if not to the same extent as among managers in the fish processing industry. If the prerequisite for increasing expertise is strengthening of the connections between firms, then it is an advantage that these connections are already so common. It should also be expected that such cooperation will result in "meta-learning," that is, the study of cooperation and of learning through cooperation. In that case, the motivational base would be laid. The spokesperson for increased expertise through network-building will not meet with communications problems, because those involved in the industry will understand what it is all about.

Network-building cannot replace measures directed towards the individual practitioners of the industry. Both types of initiative must go hand in hand. High individual expertise makes people less vulnerable in times of crisis, and gives them more to contribute in good times, to their own firm and in relation to the network. The more one has to offer others in the network, the more one can expect in return. It can therefore be said that individual-oriented efforts are prerequisites for collective initiatives to yield results.

CULTURAL COMPETENCE

Today the fishing industry is challenged by the latest in research
and technology, which represent positive opportunities. Changes
are also taking place in consumer buying. These, in turn, lead to
changes in the composition of the product and to improvements in
the treatment of the raw material. The microwave oven has become
a great challenge to the fishing industry.

These changes do not pose a threat to the coastal culture.
Whatever will make the firms more market-oriented and research-
based will also make them more interesting places to work. If the
fishermen are pessimistic and negative about their vocation today,
then the fish plant workers are not much more positive (Ivar Sagen
found that only half of the fishermen under 40 years of age would
continue in their vocation if there were alternate job opportunities
in the area). Such views represent the greatest danger to the coastal
culture.

In many ways, it is comforting to the coastal culture that we are
dealing with firms and managers of firms who are so closely attached
to their local communities. The fact that eight out of ten managers
of firms in the fish processing industry were born and raised in the
district in which the firm was located ensures a cultural expertise
which must be at the base of any changes. It also means that the
managers feel a responsibility to their local communities. Cultural
expertise is not learned in the classroom, but by growing up in a
place. It is therefore still important to have owners and managers
with local roots.

From this point of view, the many take-overs of firms by
outsiders, which are happening in the present crisis, represent a
negative trend. Bugøyenes and Brettenes are localities which have
often been mentioned in the media. The purchase of such facilities
is not necessarily done out of concern for the locality. Rather, it is
based on a desire to gain from the real values of the plants. The crisis
has caused the second-hand values of the machinery to be higher
than the price paid for a complete plant.

If this trend to "outside" take-overs follows in the wake of the
crisis, then many fishing communities will be badly off. It will pull
the rug from under many good suggestions and plans drawn from
the recommendation of the Coastal Expertise Committee. Counter-
measures are needed, not least from those responsible for management on a regional and national level. These, too, must be based on
knowledge of local ties and why they are so important.

Should the Fox Guard the Chickens?   **13**

The fisheries crisis has revealed a great reluctance on the part of fishermen to adhere to regulations. We now have the concept of "black fisheries,"[1] and there is talk about the need to establish a separate eco-criminology section for the fishing industry and for the Inspection Board to become stricter. Increased control by the police or the Board is, however, hardly a solution to the problem. If the fishermen are intent on circumventing the regulations, they cannot be stopped, no matter how strict the inspection is. It is also feared that increased monitoring and inspection will further undermine trust, because it will be seen as a provocation and encourage disobedience. The more often they break the rules, the more hardened people become.

Disregarding the law is even justified by referring to the principles of the rights of the commons. One fisherman quoted Martin Luther King when he commented to *Nordlys* (19 May 1990): "You have a moral obligation to obey just laws. But you have an equally great moral obligation to disobey unjust laws."

ECONOMIC VALUE

Trust is related to the concept of legitimacy. A legitimate power is generally trusted to the degree that rules issued by the authorities are accepted and obeyed, because they are seen to be based on reason.

We are faced here with a key problem, both in the fisheries and in society as a whole. It makes no difference how good the models for regulations are on the drawing board if the fishermen are not willing to obey them. In addition, there comes a time when the costs of inspection and supervision can no longer be justified. If the goal is to monitor the inshore fleet as thoroughly as the trawler fleet or the purse seine fleet, then the costs will be prohibitively high (Kristiansen 1985). Legitimacy thus also has economic consequences. When legitimacy is gone, the regulatory system becomes expensive because so many resources must be used to guard against law breaking. Or in professional jargon, the collective transactional costs go sky high.

We have not come so far in the Norwegian fishing industry that cheating and trickery have become part of our culture, but there is no doubt that we could get there. Bonnie McCay (1984) found that falsification of catch reports had become the normal practice in an inshore fishery on the east coast of the U.S.A. The fishermen explained their sabotage as a protest against regulations they considered unjust. They are then called "pirates" and "lawless elements" in the media and by the authorities.

The interesting point with the American example is that the negative attitude towards the authorities which has justified cheating in the minds of the fishermen has existed for generations. Little by little, it has acquired the character of a myth which has survived from one generation to the next. The myth has a real historical background, but still serves as an excuse for the fishermen's interpretation of the authorities' present actions; it is kept alive by new stories and events constantly being attached to it. And fishermen have long memories, much longer than the civil servants who come and go in the departments and who, themselves, are fed opinions of what the fishermen "are like." Thus, a foundation is laid for permanent mutual mistrust.

IMPAIRED FAITH

The legitimacy of the government is vulnerable, perhaps more so among Norwegian fishermen than among their American counterparts because, in Norway, we have traditionally had much greater expectations of the government. Foreign social scientists have observed that the government in the Scandinavian countries enjoys strong support by the population; we do not consider the government to be oppressive. (This has historical roots which will not be discussed here.)

When the expectations placed on the government are so high, however, the blow is that much harder when those expectations cannot be met. Unstable governments increase the chance of disappointment. There is a risk of breach of promise because a political party never remains in government power long enough to implement its programme. Not only do people stop believing in a particular party, but their faith in the ability of the authorities to do anything about a problem is totally lost.

One may assume that, over time, a mutual accommodation between expectation and performance will occur, until a point of equilibrium is reached. The question is, however, what may happen on the road to this, and what would such a balanced situation look like? Would it be a regulatory system which protects the fish and the fishermen from extinction?

BASIS FOR LEGITIMACY

The legitimacy of the government has been the subject of international research for many years. Social science theorists such as Joseph Schumpeter and Max Weber posed questions about the basis for legitimacy, such as, what hinders and what promotes government legitimacy? One conclusion, also supported by more recent research (Weil 1989), is that the government's actions are important enough, but are not the only things which promote legitimacy. Also important is how the decision-making process takes place. Is democracy functioning? Is it possible to voice dissenting opinions?

Defeat can be accepted as long as one has been allowed to speak up in a decision-making process which has been carried out justly. A defeat is harder to swallow if there is a feeling of having been run over by people who have not followed democratic rules of the game. If there is no fair play, then a person will not only experience negative feelings towards the decision, but will become an opponent of the system itself.

Social scientists differentiate between what they call "content legitimacy" and "procedural legitimacy." The first deals with what the regulations entail, whether they serve their purpose, function justly and are understood by those who are regulated. Procedural legitimacy deals with whether the interests concerned are being heard in the decision-making process in a manner acceptable to them. This relates particularly to how the regulatory system is organized and its openness to democracy.

Both content and procedure are important if there is a desire to promote the legitimacy of the regulations. In this chapter, however, we will discuss mainly the procedures. One point to be examined is that adherence to the law can be assured, even if the score on content legitimacy is low, as long as procedural legitimacy is maintained. The latter is no less important when discussing regulations in the fisheries. The problem can be illustrated by the use of the table shown below.

The figures in each square indicate in which of the four situations one can expect the greatest willingness to abide by the regulations. Adherence will be greatest in the square at top left and lowest in the square bottom right.

In square 1, the fishermen accept the regulations and the method by which they have come about. As mentioned, high procedural legitimacy presumes a democratic process in which the fishermen themselves have been actively involved. The fishermen will then have a feeling that they have a "right of ownership" to the regulations, with the result that they would want to both identify with them and adhere to them. At the same time, they will feel personally "betrayed" if their brethren do not. This will come as an expression of disapproval rather than opting out because the decision making process permits that.

Figure 4

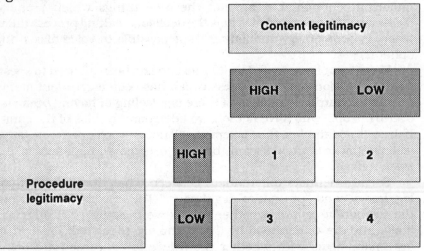

In square 4, the scoring is low in both content and procedure. Here, the fishermen are neither satisfied with the regulations nor with the methods used to develop them. Two ways of reacting are probable. First, it is reasonable to assume poor adherence to the rules. The fishermen will feel that they fool the government more than each other. Secondly, collective action can be expected. Instances of blocking harbour entrances have occurred, and are often used as a threat when the fishermen plan to protest against regulations.

The two remaining squares are most interesting. In square 3, there is a positive attitude to the content of the regulations, but a negative attitude to the procedure. This may be expressed by the fishermen refusing to be directed by bureaucrats who have a mainly theoretical view of the fisheries—"paper fishermen," as people in the Fisheries Directorate were called in Lofoten in the 1800s when the dispute about regulations was at its fiercest. In this situation, if the fishermen refuse to follow the regulations, it is the bureaucrats they fool, not each other.

In square 2, the score is high on procedural legitimacy and low on content legitimacy. Here, it is the fishermen who have critical objections to the regulations, but not to the decision-making procedure followed. They have participated in the decision-making process, but lost in a properly conducted vote.

CONSENSUS OR COMPROMISE?

There is a greater probability of the fishermen adhering to the regulations in square 2 than in square 3. Three reasons speak for that. Firstly, square 2 concerns a regular democratic process, where the normal rules of the game require the minority to give in to the majority. Secondly, the decision-making process itself makes it possible for a negative attitude to change to positive. That is because the fishermen, through discussions and negotiations, could arrive at a reasonable compromise. There is even a hope for consensus, because the parties learn to understand each other's points of view and may be convinced by them. Thirdly, it can be expected that the practical knowledge of the fishermen, as well as the overview of local conditions, would permeate the regulatory process. This could lead not only to more fairness, but also to more appropriate regulations. In other words, the procedure has a positive effect on the content because participation by the fishermen brought significant knowledge to bear on the decision-making process.

It could be argued in favour of 2 and 3 changing places in the diagram. In addition, even though high procedural legitimacy could outweigh content legitimacy, there is a limit to how low the content legitimacy may go. If the regulations are sufficiently unfair, they will be sabotaged even if the proper procedures have been followed. That does not change the conclusions we can draw thus far:
1. In order for a regulatory system to be effective, the fishermen must be involved.
2. A regulatory system will never be better than is permitted by the fishermen.

3. The fishermen will be more inclined to obey regulations if they
    have helped to formulate them.

More generally, it can be said that a regulatory system which
hinges only on content is more vulnerable and more exposed to
sabotage by fishermen than a regulatory system which also relies
on procedure.

This is not a controversial conclusion. In the Norwegian regulatory system, attempts have been made to involve fishermen in the
decision-making procedure through the Regulatory Council (Regu-
leringsrådet). The Council enables the authorities to have a basis for
more informed decisions by allowing the representatives of those
involved in the industry to have their say. At the same time, the
Regulatory Council is meant to ensure the fishermen's backing of
the regulations.

CENTRALLY CONDUCTED CONSULTATIONS

The Regulatory Council does not, however, lessen the impression of
a rather centralized regulatory system. Firstly, we have a consultation system. The name says that it is an advisory body. Secondly,
the Council speaks on regulations for the whole Norwegian zone.
This covers a large area of ocean with many types of fisheries and it
will necessarily be a great distance from the Council to the man in
the boat.

In addition, the Council is a body which includes many diverse
interests. The fishermen have five of the thirteen members. The fish
processing industry, oceanographic research and the government
also have representatives on the Council. It is therefore not surprising that there may be disagreements in and about the Council.
Often, the Council is the recipient of the fishermen's wrath.

Questions have been raised whether the Council really has a
purpose. Some even want to put most of the blame for the crisis we
are in today on the Council. Problems with this institution will
therefore be mentioned here.

One is a lack of responsibility. Those involved in the industry
could be said to have considerable influence, since the recommendations of the Council, which frequently reflect the fishermen's
position, are usually adopted. But the consultation principle frees
the Council, its members and the groups they represent from any
responsibility for the final decisions and their consequences. This
responsibility rests with the government.

Power without responsibility on the one hand, and participants
with opposing interests on the other, is not a good combination. It
opens up the negotiation game which may easily have doubtful

results. The logic of the game dictates that the industrial representatives will find themselves in the role of adversary of the
authorities, such as when subsidies are being negotiated each year.[2]
They will therefore adopt an offensive strategy.

The task of the government will then be to take a defensive
position as guardian of the fish stocks and as judge in distribution
conflicts between groups and regions. But to be defender and judge
at the same time is not easy. Here the government experiences a role
conflict. It must be tempting to put more weight on the judge's role
than on the defender's—the fish do not represent a political pressure
group as do the fishermen. The distribution conflicts may be addressed by increasing the quotas and effecting savings in transfer
payments, both of which ease the political pressure on the authorities. The fact that the fish stock estimates are uncertain and the
quota recommendations are presented as a choice between several
alternatives also makes the political problems less complicated.

NEW ORGANIZATIONAL FORMS

The built-in conflicts in the Council may speak in favour of reorgani-
zation. Instead of a national council, the tasks might be
decentralized over several councils. Decentralization would reduce
the distance between bureaucracy and the boat.

The problem of the Council giving the fishermen power without
responsibility may be solved in two ways. Firstly, all influence could
be removed from the fishermen; they could be completely locked out
of the decision-making process. I will comment on this alternative
later. The other solution is to delegate greater responsibility for
regulations to the fishermen's organizations. Decentralization and
delegation may also be combined as principles for organization of
the regulatory system. Again, we will use a four square table.

If we accept the description of the present regulatory system as
"centrally directed consultation," then we are in square 1, that is, in
the top left square. It can take us three ways: If we go to square 2,
it means delegation. It may be a solution to give more responsibility
to the Norwegian Fishermen's Association. That would mean to go
along with the arrangement which applies to the distribution of
subsidies, where the association plays an important role. But this
solution does not necessarily bring the regulatory decisions or their
makers any closer to the fishermen. As can be seen from Norwegian
newspapers, the frustration of the fishermen is directed towards the
association just as often as towards the authorities and the Regulatory Council. This is why the Norwegian Inshore Fishermen's
Association (Norges Kystfiskarlag) was established.[3]

Figure 5

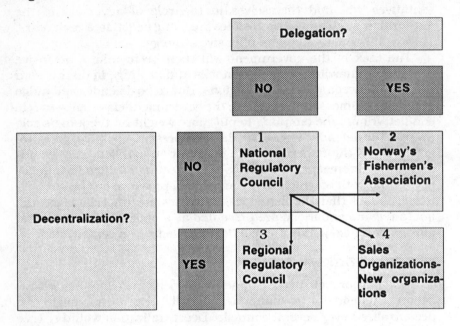

COOPERATION

If we move vertically from square 1 to square 3, that means decentralization. The decisions are now made at a lower geographic and administrative level. Such a system brings the regulatory decisions somewhat closer to home, but would be "exocratic"; the fishermen are still directed by an external authority. Here, one could envisage, like Hersoug and Hoel (1989), the provincial authorities being given more responsibility, or regional regulatory councils being established as consultative bodies, based on the present national arrangement. The Regional (Norwegian) Committee for North Norway and Namdalen (Landsdelsutvalget for Nord Norge and Namdalen) are considering something along those lines. The problem with this model is that it is easy to have the same strategic negotiation games as described in the National Council, only at a lower level.

If we move across to square 4, delegation and decentralization take place. Here, consultation is replaced by cooperation—the direction is not "exocratic" but "endocratic," that is from the inside. In other words, extensive self-regulation is practised, as is done in Lofoten.

The table indicates that fishermen's cooperative sales associations, such as the Norwegian Raw Fish Association (Norges Råfisklag) are given regulatory tasks.[4] It would not be so bad to have the pricing policy and the regulation policy coordinated. Today the raw fish price is set by what the market can bear and not in relation to what the fish stocks can tolerate.

Such a solution is practised today in some EC (European Community) countries. The British authorities distribute their national quota among cooperative sales associations, which then determine the rest. As far as is known, the arrangements have been successful; at least, the leaders of the sales associations maintain that obedience to the law has increased considerably since the fishermen themselves got control of the regulations. It is also worth noting that the ocean-going fleet is included in this arrangement. This suggests that delegating regulatory responsibility does not have to be an impossible idea for us.[5]

Another idea would be to establish new organizations for regulatory purposes, for example, "regional cooperation councils" similar to what the so-called Nylund committee suggested in 1982 (NOU 1982:5). The committee's assignment was to study measures which could contribute to a levelling out of supplies of raw material to the fish processing industry. The study report is gathering dust on a shelf in the Department of Fisheries. Some say the time was not ripe for such ideas in 1982. Maybe it is now?

THE FOX AND THE CHICKENS

In square 4 many are likely to see "the fox and the chickens," an image often invoked when the Regulatory Council is criticized, based on the supposition that the fishermen would introduce weaker regulations if they were given the responsibility. But it is likely to be the opposite. We are now back to the main point—the greater the legitimacy, the stricter the regulations the fishermen will accept. It is wrong to assume that the fishermen would misuse their authority because of their unwillingness to obey current regulations. When the fishermen go from being the adversaries to being the responsible party, their behaviour is likely to change.

As things stand today, the problem of transferring greater responsibility to the fishermen is that the crisis has contributed to a sharpening of the differences in the industry. This is not a good starting point for delegation and decentralization. There would still be a need for an external authority which could step in and solve the conflicts when they arose. Central authorities also have a role to play in the determination and distribution of the total quotas between regions or sales associations.

If the legitimacy of the current regulatory system is undermined because the government does not have the prerequisites to solve the complicated regulatory problems, then the solution cannot be to centralize still more responsibility. That would be in line with Schumpeter's argument that increased responsibility also increases the expectations of what the government can manage, and with them the chances of new disappointments. This is a quick way to get caught in a vicious circle. To avoid it, according to Schumpeter (1943, 1979), it is important both to reduce the government's responsibility and to dampen the expectations of what the government can do.

COLD WAR

There are those who feel that the regulatory responsibility should be further centralized, as well as have more detailed control. Some have come out in the open and said that dictatorship should be introduced, and that the fishermen should be removed from the decision-making process.

That would be a step in the wrong direction. Norwegian fishermen have traditionally had a positive relationship with the authorities. Not all countries experience that type of relationship. A visit to Canada, for example, could produce the strong impression that the government is seen as the "enemy" when the fishermen discuss regulations. Violent reactions to government controls have occurred, and the fishermen have even set fire to fisheries patrol boats. In response, the patrol boats have been equipped with weapons. It would be tragic if this should become the situation in the Norwegian fisheries. We would certainly have a less effective and a much more expensive regulatory system.

Centralization is the opposite of what should be done in the present situation. Democracy has its problems, but it is preferable to dictatorship. In the present situation, the fishermen must be made responsible, not lose authority. Giving them greater responsibility in a functional sense, that is, for tasks involving regulations, may lead to their becoming more responsible in a moral sense.

Does a Good Regulatory System Exist?

14

What is a good regulatory system? What considerations should be emphasized when developing a good regulatory arrangement? What should be the goal and what should be avoided at all costs? The fisheries crisis has led to an intense public debate about these questions. That opinions have diverged in all directions was only to be expected. The interests are varied and political opinion is divided. It is nevertheless essential to come to an agreement, or the system will be paralyzed and the crisis thus prolonged.

MANY CONCERNS

The list of requirements for a good regulatory system presented below has been compiled by listening to the debate, recording the statements approved by the fishermen's organizations, and reading the fisheries press. The requirements are listed in no particular order.

A good regulatory system should:

1. Prevent overfishing.
2. Reduce existing overcapacity.
3. Prevent new overcapacity.
4. Ensure effective execution of the fisheries.
5. Ensure renewal of the fleet.
6. Avoid competitive fishing and stress.
7. Ensure quality.
8. Create predictability.
9. Ensure transparency (clarity).
10. Avoid "cannibalism."

11. Ensure versatile fleet structure.
12. Prevent discards.
13. Preserve the fiord fishery.
14. Protect Saami interests.
15. Ensure regional distribution.
16. Ensure historical shares.
17. Ensure fairness.
18. Ensure equal treatment.
19. Spread out the fishery over the year.
20. Ensure freedom/flexibility.
21. Avoid "skipper" fishing.
22. Preserve employment.
23. Ensure recruitment to the trade.
24. Reward the best.
25. Avoid anyone becoming a loser.
26. Avoid creating elitist groups.
27. Avoid crews becoming "tenant farmers."
28. Avoid privatization of the commons.
29. Ensure support/legitimacy.
30. Avoid splitting local communities.
31. Counter cheating and "black fishing."
32. Prevent speculation.
33. Avoid artificial creation of value.
34. Ensure control of (total) catch.
35. Tolerate variations in the total amount.
36. Tolerate variations in availability.
37. Ensure that the total quota is taken.
38. Ensure business profitability.
39. Ensure socio-economic profitability.
40. Reduce inspection costs.
41. Reduce the bureaucracy.
42. Avoid detailed regulations.
43. Avoid precedent-setting incidents.
44. Give priority to the most fisheries-dependent.
45. Maintain excitement in the fisheries.
46. Avoid weakening safety.
47. Survive joining the European Community.
48. Protect part-time fishermen.
49. Give preference to full-time fishermen.
50. Limit sports fishing.
51. Make possible a good family life.
52. Simplify administration.
53. Avoid splitting the Fishermen's Association.

This can safely be said to be a rather long list, and still it is not likely to be complete. The unavoidable question which comes to mind is: is there any possibility of developing a regulatory system which takes into account all the considerations listed above? That is doubtful. To date, no country has developed such a regulatory system, so the Norwegian government should not be criticized for not having come up with the ultimate solution. Instead it should be praised for having proceeded cautiously instead of slavishly following fashionable international fluctuations. One might oppose transferable quotas, but cannot dispute the fact that the authorities have studied the issue.

Many of the considerations listed above overlap. If one is ensured, then the other is well on the way to being ensured. Some depend on others; they must be realized at the same time. But to have one's cake and eat it too may be difficult with regard to some of these points. For example: a regulatory system which rewards quality encourages discards. If the fishery were regulated so that it were spread out evenly over the year, that would benefit the fish processing industry and those fishermen who traditionally start their season later than others. But such periodization would cause increased expenses to the fishermen because they would have to re-equip for other types of fishing more frequently. Another example: the same quota for all would mean equal treatment and simplified administration. But this could easily be seen as unfair because some have new boats and large debts, while others have old boats which have been paid for. Equal cod quotas for all would also hurt those who have few alternate resources to fall back on.

The challenge consists in developing a regulatory system which makes it possible to reconcile as many as possible of such opposites, if not completely, then at least in good part.

AGREEMENT

When faced with the choice between conflicting concerns, it is tempting to answer as Winnie the Pooh did when he was asked whether he wanted milk or honey: "Yes please, both." The matter would be easier if decisions were made about which concerns should take precedence over others. All the considerations are not likely to be equally important. One could probably live with some of the problems. Is it more important, equally important or less important to increase efficiency than to ensure employment? Is it more important, equally important or less important to keep the commons open than to protect the fiord fishery for the benefit of those living in the fiords? Is it more important to maintain competition than to give

priority to quality, reliability and predictability? The questions could
go on and on. The more purposes a regulatory system is to serve,
the more complex it becomes. It would be difficult to have a single
regulatory system for the whole fleet. Maybe several regulatory
systems are needed, either in combination with each other simulta-
neously or by gradually moving from one system to another as total
quotas increase. Perhaps different regulations should be put into
effect for different segments of the fleet—maximum quotas for some,
vessel quotas for others, saleable quotas for the third, seasonal
quotas for the fourth, and so on. It might even be worth considering
introducing different regulatory systems for different regions of the
country. It should not be taken for granted that the fishermen in
Finnmark should be regulated in the same manner as the fishermen
in Trøndelag or Sørlandet.

Experts in the Fisheries Directorate and the various research
environments can give help in technically structuring a regulatory
system that meets all the requirements placed on it. But deciding
which of the above considerations is most important is not a matter
for the experts. That is a political matter. The concerns relate to
values; what we value highly, what we feel important as goals for
development in the fishing regions. The fishermen are not the only
ones who have the right to a say in this matter, but they have more
right than others because they are the most affected.

The matter of regulation is not only what system functions best,
but also how to achieve *agreement* as to what constitutes a good
regulatory system, that is, which of the above considerations should
be used as a base and how should they be prioritized. The problem
is that some are winners and some are losers, depending on the
method of regulation. That is the case when there is a choice
between, for example, maximum quotas or vessel quotas. The challenge thus is not only to create a good regulatory system, as such,
but also to create a good decision-making process which can unite
opposites and achieve compromises. Two requirements must be
placed on this decision-making process. Firstly, it must be reason-
ably rational. Secondly, it must be as democratic as possible.
Unfortunately, there may be a conflict between these two requirements, but it is not possible to meet one and neglect the other.

RATIONALITY

A rational decision-making process would start with a discussion of
concerns the regulatory system should focus on. The means cannot
be discussed before the goals have been clarified. The list I have

presented should be reviewed and the points ranked according to their importance.

Some concerns are discovered only after experience has been gained. Who could have predicted that the vessel quota arrangement introduced in 1990 would have resulted in skippers laying off crews and taking turns on each other's boats? Thus the requirement that the regulations must prevent development of skipper fishing is new. A completely rational decision-making process presumes that one can predict such effects, but it is only in the world of theory that all consequences of all alternatives can be foreseen.

So it is not unreasonable to say: "We have studied and discussed the matter long enough, now we will make a decision." It is then important to monitor the effects of the regulatory system, to learn from experience and to remember the problems which the old regulatory system was intended to solve, before discarding it and introducing something completely new.

It is also important not to be too confident. Connections between issues are not always as unambiguous as they might appear. If, for example, vessel quotas, and not maximum quotas, are selected out of concern for quality, then one must be certain that vessel quotas actually will have this effect, and that it is not the good availability of fish which actually improves quality. It has also been maintained that quality suffers from reduced crewing—a result of the vessel quota arrangement—because the treatment of the fish on board lowers the quality of the landed product. (The fish is carelessly bled and gutting takes longer.) In addition, a change in attitude has taken place among the net fishermen with regard to quality. In other words, it is not certain that a maximum quota arrangement would have the same negative effect on quality today as it had some years ago. Furthermore, in the final analysis, quality depends on the inspectors doing their job.

DEMOCRACY

The argument that the decision-making process should be democratic was discussed in a previous chapter and need not be further belaboured except to reiterate that first of all, it is necessary to mobilize all the experience, knowledge and imagination in the industry. It should not be assumed that all such qualities available to the industry can be found only in the Fisheries Directorate, in the Department of Fisheries or in research environments. Secondly, it can be expected that the fishermen will, to a greater degree, identify with and live by the regulatory systems they have helped to develop.

The next question will require more attention: what kind of democracy? How to organize the decision-making process so that not only a decision, but also agreement, is reached? As mentioned, the trouble is that what is a solution for some is a problem for others. Skipper fishing saves the boat for the skipper but, at the same time, forces the crews to apply for unemployment benefits.

March and Olsen (1989) differentiate between two forms of democratic treatment. One is called *aggregation*, the other *integration*. Aggregation is a decision-making process in which the interested parties are listened to, in which they deliver their demands; when the demands are conflicting, a body at a higher level tries to reach a compromise. This may involve several stages. For example, when a provincial fishermen's association requests comments from its local associations regarding the regulations, they consolidate these and present them to the national board of the Norwegian Fishermen's Association which, in turn, makes a decision based on comments received from other provincial associations and group organizations (Norwegian Trawler Owners Association, Seine Fishermen's Association, Fishing Boat Owners Association). The problem with aggregation processes is that they may not necessarily result in agreement. Nobody need be satisfied with the final decision. The final compromise arrived at may have only the support of a majority of the national board.

The other process is democracy by integration. Here the emphasis is on active participation and broad discussion and it is not only the heavyweights who swing the vote. Instead, the important thing is for people to agree. Efforts are made to reach a consensus, not just a compromise. The interests and viewpoints of the minority are given due consideration. The participants display solidarity and take responsibility for each other. The process enables the participants to gain some insight into the reasons why their adversaries think as they do. If the situation calls for it, and the process allows it, the minority may be able to convince the majority to change sides.

The choice of decision-making methods—aggregation or integration—by the Norwegian Fishermen's Association could require a study since many of the preconditions for regulatory policy are set here. At present there are indications that the aggregation process has a tendency to win out over the integration process. The figures show that the province of Finnmark has lost a great deal since the vessel quota arrangement was introduced. When looking at the past decade, the results appear almost catastrophic (Hersoug and Hoel 1991). Nordland province, on the other hand, has fared relatively well from the regulations in recent years, and the same can be said for the provinces further south. One test of whether aggregation or integration occurs would be if the Fishermen's Association could agree internally on a regulatory system which could rectify the treatment of Finnmark province. So far this has not happened; any suggestion along that line has been voted down.

NATURAL LAW

Anyone who insists on the principle of an open commons avoids taking a stand on the actual distribution between regions and groups. In the beginning, support is given to the result of free competition, whatever that may be. If Finnmark province loses, that is the judgement of the market. During the fisheries crisis, however, questions have been raised as to whether the population of Finnmark, including the Saami population, can be said to have an inherent right to the fish resources in their area. If so, then it is fundamental rights which are being violated when the province gets the "wrong end of the stick."

The problem is of a general nature: what forms the basis for rights to, for example, natural resources? Discussion of this topic has given rise to what the philosophers and lawyers call natural law. The ancient philosophers insisted that laws and regulations had to be founded on morality, on principles of what is just.

Natural law, in this view, goes deeper than the rights encoded in laws and regulations. It is in line with the natural law perspective to insist that dependency makes rights legitimate. When the government, in the Coastal Notice (Parliamentary report No. 32, 1990–91), proposed that the most fisheries-dependent regions should be given preference, it is basically a principle of natural law that is being advocated.

Note that this deviates from other principles which are often used in the fishing industry, for example, that the cleverest, the most industrious and the luckiest have a right to a larger portion of the resources than do others. It is also different from the principle underlying the idea of transferable quotas, that is, that one has a right to what one can afford. The latter is a reasonable rule when we go shopping in the grocery store, but during the debate about saleable quotas it became clear that many find this unacceptable when applied to fish resources.

FISHERIES DEPENDENCY

The figures from the province of Finnmark indicate that the goal of prioritizing the most fisheries-dependent regions is easier to espouse than to put into practice. Evidence of this also comes from Nordland province, where one may check the success of a policy aimed at favouring the most fisheries-dependent municipalities by taking a trip to the outermost islands like Værøy and Røst. Even though they are hit by the crisis as are other places, one would expect that by comparison with less fisheries-dependent municipalities they would be fairly well off (having been favoured by policy). However, Værøy and Røst are the two municipalities which, in the 1980s, had the largest decrease in population of all the municipalities in the province of Nordland. On Røst, the population decreased by over 21 percent, on Værøy by almost 17 percent.

How this decline can "retain the main features of the settlement pattern," the goal of the regional policy for many years now, is uncertain given the ambiguity of the goal. But there is no doubt that drastic measures are required to reverse the development as regards the most fisheries-dependent municipalities.

In defence of the authorities it may be said that attempts have been made to favour the most fisheries-dependent regions to a certain degree. Regional quotas and small-trawl licences to the province of Finnmark are good examples. These measures, however, met with sharp resistance from southern fishermen and were considerably modified as a result. It should be noted that the harshest criticism came from groups within the fishing industry and not from the outside.

There is therefore probably no great cause for optimism on the part of the most fisheries-dependent municipalities. We will probably manage to rebuild the fish resources and we will, hopefully, manage to agree on which principles and goals should take precedence in fisheries policy. On the other hand, some pessimism is justifiable with regard to practical implementation. There is every reason to fear that action will be paralyzed by disagreement as to the means.

Is There Any Hope?   15

Nobody knows what the future will bring, particularly for the fishing industry. But we now know a good deal about where we stand and what has brought us here. And we can say with certainty that if the development along the coast continues as it has done up to now, then the worst is yet to come.

People must have faith in the future or it will bode ill for the coastal culture. Stark pessimism nevertheless rules today. How is it possible to hope for better times when one cannot even dangle a line over the side? To be an optimist, one must be convinced that something can be done about the situation. As has been argued in this book, knowledge and expertise are required—knowledge of nature and ecology, as well as of technology and marketing. But optimism also requires a belief that the crisis can be dealt with on a political level. The choices we are faced with are difficult because, among other things, they question our fundamental values and goals for the development of society. Can the coastal population trust the authorities to choose correctly?

ON AN EVEN KEEL?

The Coastal Notice (Parliamentary Report, No. 32, 1990–91, "On an Even Keel" ["På rett kjøl"]) which was submitted in the spring of 1991 provides an updated description of conditions in the fishing districts. The figures presented are nothing to get excited about. They show that the most fisheries-dependent municipalities have experienced a greater decrease in population than all other municipalities in Norway for the period of 1970 to 1990. The department is painting the devil on the wall: "If the pattern of migration of youth from the outports of coastal Norway during the 1970s and 1980s should continue, the generation of young adults in the fishing municipalities will be halved by the year 2010" (p. 15).

According to the Notice, the most fisheries-dependent municipalities are burdened with the highest unemployment, the greatest number of people on disability pensions, the greatest debt, and the lowest revenue from taxes per inhabitant. The further north, the worse the picture. The most sombre situation is in the province of Finnmark, where dependence on the fisheries is the greatest.

The statistics clearly show the reason for the problems in the most fisheries-dependent municipalities. Fishing activities have been displaced from the north to the south. "The North Norwegian fleet's share of the total catch of all species of fish has been reduced from a good 32 percent in 1977 to 23 percent in 1989" (p. 33). Again, the figures show that Finnmark has been bled the most.

In 1977, Norway established the 200-mile zone, arguing that it was essential in order to ensure the existence of the most fisheries-dependent districts. If the zone was necessary, it has certainly not proven to have been sufficient. The Coastal Notice said it clearly: "Should this development continue, then the region (North Norway) is in danger of having its share further reduced, even in a more normal resource situation" (p. 33). The crisis in the north then, will not necessarily end in 1995. To reverse the trend, more is needed than restoration of the fish stock. The allocation processes must also be examined.

NORTH AND SOUTH

There are many differing interests in the Norwegian fishing industry; they go far back in history and are often played out as a north-south conflict. That is one of the reasons the industry is characterized by a complex and fragmented organizational pattern. It does not help that the lines of conflict cross each other. A conflict between sea and land (in the matter of on-board production), between the ocean-going fleet and the inshore fleet and between fish processors and exporters, is, at the same time, a conflict between the north and south of the country. However, there are exceptions to the rule that on-board producers, the ocean-going fleet and the fish exporters are all located in the south.[1]

Any problem involving different regional interests is difficult to solve. Such conflicts paralyse action by political parties and national interest organizations. It is not for nothing that the political parties release their representatives when the Norwegian Parliament (Storting) has to vote on questions of great local interest (such as the location of the new aviation museum).

National (Norwegian) interest organizations have similar problems. The (Norwegian) Fishermen's Association (Norges Fiskarlag)
has always insisted on no discrimination between fishermen by
region. A fisherman is a fisherman, regardless of where he lives.
Anything else would, of necessity, be seen as unfair by the members
and be inimical to the feeling of solidarity in the organization. It was
therefore to be expected that, in its response to the Coastal Notice,
the Fishermen's Association said it "will strongly disassociate itself
from any hint of regional management of the resource."

It appears to be easier to agree on regional-neutral criteria, such
as the Fishermen's Association distribution of income subsidies
(even if it can be proven that the regional distribution effect is
skewed). The Coastal Notice repeats what has been known for a long
time:

> Even if the high level of government transfers is legitimized based
> on domicile, there is little which reflects the actual distribution of
> the funds. The most fisheries-dependent regions of the country
> have—possibly with the exception of very recent years—received a
> clearly lower proportion of the fisheries subsidy funds than the
> absolute level of fisheries employment and the industry's relative
> importance to the total employment in these areas would dictate
> (p. 46).

The explanation for this paradoxical phenomenon is that the
subsidies have been issued mainly as supplements to the price the
fishermen received for their catch. Whoever catches the most fish
gets the most support. How much fish one catches depends a great
deal on the size of the vessel, and since the largest vessels are
generally found in the south, this region receives more subsidies
than North Norway where the inshore fleet dominates (Jentoft and
Mikalsen 1987).

Since the fisheries economist Bjørn Brochmann pointed it out
in the early 1980s, it has been accepted that the fisheries subsidy
has contributed to the over-capacity in the fishing fleet which ruined
the resource base and brought the coastal municipalities into crisis
(Brochmann 1981). The quote from the Coastal Notice leads to the
logical conclusion that the uneven distribution of support has also
contributed to a development which, since the 200-mile zone was
established, has been hardest on the fishing communities in the
north.

NATIONAL RESOURCE?

Regional quotas and decentralization of the management system
have been suggested by, among others, the Regional Committee for

North Norway and Namdalen, in order to reestablish the historic distribution between regions of the country. Of course, the suggestion has caused dissension, not least between North Norway and Vestlandet. Opponents of regionalization have argued that the fish is a "national resource." This principle is understood to exclude regionalization. Even the Norwegian Fishermen's Association maintained as much in its presentation at the hearings on the Coastal Notice.

In the political debate about rights in the fisheries, it is strongly argued that fish is a national property. Those maintaining anything different have a much weaker case, unless, like the Saami, they can point to some common or more fundamental reasons than the rights to the fish resources. (There have been few objections to special consideration of the Coastal Saami population in the fisheries regulations.)

The problem, however, is that the argument about common property actually can be said to include all forms of discrimination among fishermen. Thus it comes down heavily on the present regulatory arrangements. Discrimination is precisely what the licensing system and quota arrangements practise. We now have the concept of "licence aristocracy," and it is probably only a matter of time before the concept "quota aristocracy" becomes common as well. (In Iceland they now speak of "quota kings"!) Not everybody is elevated to the peerage. Yet no one has protested against this with reference to the fish resources being a national resource. If that were the case, the fishermen who are locked out because they have fished too little in the course of the last three-year period to be granted a quota, should be able to cite their citizenship as justification.

An interpretation more in line with practice would be that "national resource" must mean that state authorities have the exclusive right to determine how the fisheries should be managed, including how the resources should be allocated geographically. In principle, there is no difference in discriminating between regions than between groups, for which there is a long tradition. In both cases, the State exercises its authority to determine how the national property right to the resources within the 200-mile zone will be administered.

It should be added that nothing in the "nature" of the fish determines that it is a national and not a regional resource. Just as it was an international resource before the introduction of 200-mile zones, the fish is what the authorities make it. The fact that it swims is not a barrier to regionalization, but it is a complication which applies to all levels, not just regional.

EFFECTIVE RHETORIC

"It must not be the mailing address which determines who deserves a quota or not." Opponents of regionalization argue that it goes against all understanding of common fairness and principles of a constitutional state. The problem is, though that regardless how one twists and turns it, some will lose and some will gain by the regulation of the fisheries, at least in the short run. It is cold comfort to those who lose out from regionalization that the nation as a whole will perhaps gain from it as a way to reduce transfer payments to the industry or avoid aid packages to Finnmark. When looked at in this light, there is no basis to moralize over protests by potential losers.

The figures in the Coastal Notice show that the development of the fisheries has already produced winners and losers—but without the authorities having identified them ahead of time. Instead, it is the market mechanism that followed the "mailing address principle." Naturally, there are greater worries in the north than in the south. The opponents of regionalization could therefore be asked if they have a negative view of the principle itself, or whether they are only sceptical of the authorities governing in accordance with it.

Whoever can point to common principles and values in the distribution conflicts argues from a stronger position than those who have only self-interest as a defence. Statements such as "fish is a national resource" are effective rhetoric. Champions of preserving the inshore fleet as the "backbone of the settlement pattern" have always been defenceless against the claim that technological development, either in the fisheries or in other industries, cannot be stopped. Technology has given us a catching capacity which far exceeds what the resource base can tolerate. It has also resulted in the most fisheries-dependent regions lagging behind because the inshore fishery has suffered.

Similarly, those who today fight for the coastal culture are vulnerable to arguments that it is a socio-economic "waste" to have 25,000 fishermen, when 7,000 are sufficient—as was calculated in a recently presented publicly funded study (Førsund *et al.* 1991). A reference to the high unemployment in society as a whole will have only a temporary effect. The day the unemployment figures drop, other arguments must be brought forward. But any change in argument just gives the impression of hidden motives. Could there be other arguments of more lasting value to the advantage of the most fisheries-dependent coastal districts?

SUSTAINABLE DEVELOPMENT

The World Commission for Environment and Development, the Brundtland Commission (1987), has given us a new concept—"sustainable development"—on which to base fisheries policy. It is at the centre of a number of parliamentary reports about nature, the environment and district policies that have been published in recent years (see, for example, Parliamentary Report, No. 29, 1988–89, Parliamentary Report, No. 46, 1988–89). The Coastal Notice is no exception. As the concept is defined by the Brundtland commission, it concerns far more than ecology and economy; it also deals with democracy and culture.

One problem is that ecological crises invite centralization of power and control. They could lead to removing authority from those who make a living from harvesting the resources. Local knowledge would be pushed aside by scientific knowledge, and people would find that their lives were subjected to forces over which they had no control. In other words, a society which takes ecological problems seriously risks becoming an authoritarian society.

The Brundtland Commission is aware of this dilemma. Spokespersons for regionalization of fisheries management should, for example, find comfort in the following:

> What is needed most is that the population have the knowledge and the will to follow up, which means the population being allowed to participate in the decisions which will affect the environment. This is best achieved by decentralization of control of the resources which the local population is dependent on, and by providing the population with real input into how these resources should be used (p. 18).

Sustainable development is an expression of common sense which most find obvious. But like other common principles often referred to in fisheries policy, this, too, has a distribution aspect. Regionalization—which means, among other things, "to decentralize control of the resources"—is one of the many examples. A demand for a less energy-intensive fishery, which is also in line with the principle of sustainable development, would be in the interest of the inshore fleet, and thereby also in the interest of North Norway. The same would be the case if the exploitation pattern were turned to sexually mature fish. It is also sustainable to regulate the fisheries according to a "multi-species model." But if the capelin is spared as food for the cod, the purse seine fleet, which is at present located mainly in two municipalities in the southern Vestlandet region—Austevoll and Herøy—would be hurt.

The principle of sustainable development is easy to support. It is far more difficult to agree on what it would mean in practice. Not only must there be agreement about what is sensible, but also about what is fair. On this question, winners and losers will normally part ways.

THE WILL IS THERE, BUT WHAT ABOUT THE ABILITY?

The Brundtland Commission recognizes the problem. "We are not saying that the process is simple. It is difficult to choose. The core is that lasting sustainable development must be built on political will" (p. 18). If we are to believe the Coastal Notice, then the authorities are not short on will. But what about ability? Is it possible to create sufficient legitimacy for real sustainable development when the potential losers are better organized and have greater influence on policy than do the winners?

The Brundtland Commission emphasizes the need for institutional reforms, both on an international and a national level. In particular, laws, rules and organizations must be developed which not only take into account the effects of environmental problems, but also attack the causes. Before being adopted, however, institutional reforms must go through a democratic process in which influence can be exerted through "corporate channels," that is, through interest organizations. When they turn thumbs down, political courage is needed to stick to one's guns.

The coastal crisis has shown that the authorities can be pressured. When special measures are promoted to the advantage of the most fisheries-dependent districts, they are often opposed. An example of this was the Department of Fisheries (Norway) proposal to give priority to North Norwegian trawlers when allocating quotas for the capelin fisheries in 1991. At the conclusion of the hearings, the department had to back down. This led the member of parliament from Sogn and Fjordane province to comment smugly, "Vestlandet should now have won the fight against regionalization" (*Sunnmøreposten* 5 December 1990).

Thus the distribution of provincial quotas of winter capelin was predictable. In total, Finnmark got 7.3 percent of the catch, while the fleet from Møre and Romsdal and Hordaland got a total of 61 percent (Randa and Aslaksen 1991).

This, and similar examples, suggests that people in the most fisheries-dependent districts should not hold great hopes that effective political steps will be taken towards more sustainable development—in the broad sense the Brundtland Commission interprets the concept. When looked at this way, there does not appear to be much hope that the disappointing trends outlined to in the Coastal Notice will be reversed in the next few years.

WILL THE INSTITUTIONS COLLAPSE?

The latest suggestions are for the liberalization of a series of laws and rules important to coastal societies. The Raw Fish Act—popularly known as the "Fishermen's Constitution"—which has for more than half a century acted as a buffer for the fishermen against fluctuations in their incomes, is now slated for "modernization."[2] Another idea being promoted is to introduce transferable quotas, which would reduce participation in the fisheries. A third example is that, just before the summer of 1991, the Norwegian Parliament (Storting) decided to ease the requirements contained in the regulations of the Fish Farming Licensing Act, which had ensured district-by-district dispersion and local control of the fish farming industry. Up to that time, the majority shareholders had to be local owners; now, outsiders can own the controlling interest.

Such ideas are opposed in the industry. In its statement on the Coastal Notice, the Fishermen's Association rejected the proposed changes to the Raw Fish Act, noting that "it had been a long and hard fight for the fishermen before they managed to remove the 'crofter's mark' fifty years ago and won the right to first-hand sale of their own raw material." The Norwegian Coastal Fishermen's Association (Norges Kystfiskarlag) said in a press release[3] that "saleable quotas would remove the coastal people's historic right to harvest and live off the fisheries resources." The Norwegian Fish Farmers Association (Norske Fiskeoppdretteres Forening) said, "What the fish farmers fear is that in a few years speculators will earn big money from the industry, while the people along the coast who have built it up, will end up empty-handed."[4]

Some consider these suggestions to be part of an adaptive process in preparation for the EC (European Community). Others see the changes in relation to society's generally increasing belief in the market mechanism and a process which should be implemented regardless of the form of European association. In view of the vulnerable situation in which the coastal population now finds itself, this, however, is a step in an unexpected direction. There *are* arguments in favour of the reforms suggested here. Changes in the Raw Fish Act are meant to encourage improved quality of the raw material. The intention of transferable quotas is to eliminate the overcapacity of the fleet and reduce the bureaucracy, while revisions of the Fish Farming Act will ease the supply of capital to this industry. There may be a need for all this. But, regardless of how well-founded these suggestions may be, their timing is not good.

GREAT OPPORTUNITIES

One can and should insist that the policy provide rights to those dependent on it; one should nevertheless be prepared for many to turn a deaf ear. It is important not to expect that basic conditions will be altered in the desired direction. The fate of the coast is sealed by the development of the fisheries, not necessarily by the State. While people in the most fisheries-dependent districts should work actively to have unfair laws and rules changed, they must recognize that they may not achieve their goal.

One way of increasing the odds in their favour—which has been the main theme of this book—is to increase expertise. In an age of bio- and computer technology, the plants and those involved in the industry must increase their technical qualifications. This will strengthen their ability to compete, both nationally and internationally. What is needed here is what the Coastal Expertise Committee has pointed out and what our studies have found—an all-out effort. A table in the governmental Coastal Notice shows that the educational level is lower in the fisheries-dependent municipalities than in all other municipalities, and that it gets lower the further north along the coast one goes (with the exception of the fishing districts in Trøndelag which rank the lowest).

Despite the crisis, there are also many positive possibilities. According to the marine scientists, there is an enormous potential in better management of the fisheries resources. In the crisis year 1990, the Norwegian cod quota was 113,000 metric tonnes. Norwegian marine researchers estimated the maximum long-term yield at 950,000 metric tonnes (marine researcher Johannes Hamre as quoted by Ola Flåten 1990). We must be prepared to share half with the Russians but, even so, it does say something about the profits that may be within reach. In addition to the possibilities regarding wild fish stocks, there are the great future prospects in fish farming. Researchers predict a dramatic increase in production volume as results of new research into ocean ranching are put to use.

The Coastal Expertise Committee is of the opinion that it is quite realistic to double many times the value we now take from the sea. "An increase in present Kroner value from 15 billion to 30–50 billion over a 10-year period is within practical reach." This presumes, however, that we not only become better at managing the fish resources, but also at increasing their value. The latter is less dependent on the authorities than the former. Further processing and improvement in quality are the key words. This must be primarily a local effort at sea and in the plants. Considerable barriers to such investment may be removed by an EC (European Community) agreement which will provide us with duty-free access to our most important markets.

COURAGE TO FORGE AHEAD

There is worldly wisdom in the saying, "There is always hope in a dangling line!" One must not become discouraged; whoever is patient will be rewarded. In the present situation, this idea is encouraging. But the saying also implies that it is sufficient to be passive and expectant. As advice to the coastal population, that is misleading. If there is one thing that must *not* be done these days, it is to remain inactive. Not only patience, but also courage to forge ahead is now required. Without it, the coast will have no future.

This presumes that the plants and those involved in the industry will be provided with opportunities to utilize and further develop their own potential, resources and knowledge. For this to happen some laws and regulations will have to be changed. Not all institutions are worth preserving. For instance, the 1990 amendments to the Fish Export Act were a step in the right direction. Now the plants can freely export their own products—a new opportunity, particularly for the plants in the north. If the most fisheries-dependent districts in Norway are capable of grasping this opportunity, then their future should look brighter.

We got lucky. It turned out that the fisheries crisis did not last as long as many had feared, after all. By the fall of 1992 it appeared that we had ridden out the storm. Reports by the oceanographers on fish populations in the Barents Sea in 1992 were as surprising as they had been in September 1989. But this time the message was encouraging: The fry production has never been so good since measurements were begun in 1965, reported chief of research Arvid Hylen. The situation also looked very good for pollack and haddock, while the capelin population showed a decline.

This report was, of course, well received. "The outlook has rarely been better," according to *Fiskarbladet's* editorial of September 10. "It's full speed ahead," said the Minister of Fisheries Oddrun Pettersen in her farewell speech. "We may now be optimists, but there are still reasons to be cautious," commented her successor, Jan Henry T. Olsen (*Nordlys*, 10 September). Even in the future, a strict fishery regime in the North is necessary. "The goal is still long-term: we must build up the populations so that they can survive larger and more stable quotas in the future," says Olsen. After several meetings of the Regulatory Council during the fall, the cod quota (the Norwegian share) was set at 248,000 metric tonnes for 1993, more than doubling the quota for 1990.

THE RUSSIAN CONNECTION

There were still some clouds on the horizon. The collapse of the Soviet Union led to disintegration in the Russian fisheries regulatory system and now, at beginning of 1993, Russian over-fishing is of great concern to the Norwegian authorities. Fish has become hard currency for the Russians, and Norwegians, along with other foreign fish producers, are more than willing to buy. Russian supplies have, in fact, contributed to keeping the wheels turning in the Norwegian fishing industry while the crisis lasted. The problem now is that the Russian cod, which had previously been consumed at home, is causing lower prices for both the fishermen and the fish producers. For the first time in living memory the Lofoten season began with buyers holding back.

In other words, just when the resources appear to be improving, the market is deteriorating. When prices fall and the control of the catches is poor, the black market opens up and creates problems in keeping a proper overview of the harvest of the resources. Many people in the fishing industry predict a new crisis within a few years. The Russian supplies cannot be expected to last.

The situation is no less uncertain in the fish farming industry. Many predicted that it would collapse and this happened in the fall of 1991. Attempts to limit the volume of sales by storing frozen fish misfired and the prices have been in a free fall ever since. The Fish Farmers Sales Organization (Fiskeoppdretternes Salgslag—FOS) landed in court and a large number of fish farmers, particularly in Northern Norway, were left with great losses which they cannot cover. With the bankruptcy of FOS, the opportunity to stabilize the price level through coordinated production and sale is seriously weakened, and the will to cooperate is no longer what it was.

The EC agreement, which should provide reductions in customs duties for important fish products, has not come into force and there is some doubt that it ever will. In the meantime, Norwegian authorities have applied for full membership in the European Community. Now, as in 1972 (the last time Norway applied for membership), the fishery is the most contentious issue. The prospect of Norway having to transfer management control of fisheries resources to EC authorities meets with strong opposition along the coast. Once the results of the negotiations are presented, membership will be decided by a popular vote. At the moment, opinion polls indicate that, once again, the majority will be against Norway becoming a member.

NEW OPTIMISM

Despite the uncertainty attached to the resource situation, the falling prices and the future market relationship, people in the industry see some light at the end of the tunnel. Again, the comments are mainly optimistic. If things go the way the researchers predict this time, then there is reason to expect better days.

The fishing industry cannot survive without optimism. But optimism has a tendency to obscure structural problems in the industry. Nobody has time to discuss what the fisheries crisis has taught us. The crisis is in the past, it is the future that matters now.

Foresight is a rare quality. People in the fishing industry cannot be expected to be any more clairvoyant than others. It should not be held against them that they listened to the promises of researchers and speeches by the Minister of Fisheries Bjarne Mørk Eidem about the growth of the industry. They had reason to have great hopes for better times towards the end of the 1980s. It was to be expected that many felt disappointed and bitter when a crisis appeared instead.

Maybe one should have expected a greater degree of "déjà vu" when the crisis occurred. Déjà vu is a feeling that something has happened before—without this actually being the case. The concept does not quite cover our situation—in the fishing industry it has actually happened. Crises are nothing new in the Norwegian fishing industry. They come and go and, even though things are now better, periods of decline will come again.

It is actually strange that the outlook among people in the industry is so pessimistic. One would think they would be mentally prepared for crises. The explanation may be that they have unrealistic expectations of the fisheries, that they assume that stability and equilibrium, and not fluctuations, are the norm in the fishing industry.

If that is the case, it is not only people in the industry who believe this. The belief that stability and equilibrium are achievable has characterized public regulatory policy in the post-war period and it did not diminish after the resource crisis started to appear towards the end of the 1960s. Researchers have supported this view: if only we knew more, then we would be able to manage the fish resources in a manner which would ensure high and lasting yields.

PANTA REI—"ALL IS FLUX"

The idea of equilibrium and stability has been the basis for the industrialization of the industry: Stable raw material supplies were both the prerequisite and the goal of the fishing industry. The inshore fleet was considered incapable of satisfying this need and ocean-going trawlers were acquired which could track down the fish, regardless of where it might be. The development in Finnmark was greatly influenced by this decision.

This perspective also characterized the public debate about the problems in the industry. When the fishery fails, then it is the authorities who have failed. Now that the cod stock is improving, the authorities are taking the credit for it. That this may be related to increased ocean temperatures, as stated by ocean researchers, is barely mentioned. That is not the way they looked at it in the old days. The expression "there is always hope in a dangling line" originates from a period when people felt that powers other than the government were masters of the fish in the ocean.

No doubt it would have been better if total control over the resources had been possible. Planning would be better, employment more secure, markets simpler to serve and investments less risky. But recent experience dictates that this is wishful thinking: "Panta rei"—all is flux, nothing is stationary, said the Greek philosopher Heraclitus. The fishing industry is clearly no exception. Rough seas and bad weather are the norm, or to use a cliché, the only stable thing in the industry is instability.

There is little indication that the crisis we have gone through has resulted in any fundamental changes in the perspective of the fishing industry and fisheries policy, either by the authorities, the industry itself or among researchers. Déjà vu does not characterize their comments at present. The central question in the wake of the crisis is nevertheless: What is rational behaviour and policy in an industry where everything fluctuates rapidly and unforeseeably?

POSITIVE ATTITUDES

An industry destined to live with fluctuations and uncertainty is not a gloomy prospect for the future. On the contrary, it may be an attractive picture provided that extreme fluctuations and their social costs can be avoided. If this were to happen, variety would increase the excitement of working in the industry. Change is interesting, routine is boring. Even though it goes up and down, the fishing industry has a large underutilized potential. Exciting challenges await the person who will take a chance. Minister of External Affairs Thorvald Stoltenberg's proposal that a Barents region be established which would create stronger contacts eastwards, must be fascinating to anyone involved in the development of the fisheries in the North. The fishing industry has everything a young person with a bit of get-up and go could wish for.

Increased expertise in all fields and at all levels will, however, be a requirement. For example, in the future it will be important to learn Russian. There is no longer a lack of good educational opportunities for those who might want to venture into the fishing industry. Today, with the Norwegian College of Fishery Science (Norges Fiskerihøgskole) in Tromsø it is even possible to get a doctorate in fisheries studies. To seek higher education is not, as before, the equivalent of a career outside the fishing industry and away from one's home port.

One would therefore expect that there would be great interest among youth in entering colleges and universities to study fisheries subjects. However, applications to the Norwegian College of Fishery Science (Norges Fiskerihøgskole) have been low. There may be a weakness at the lower levels. There is such low recruitment to fisheries education in secondary schools that the number of places in the schools have been reduced in recent years.

During the 1970s, colleagues at the University of Tromsø pointed out that the elementary schools had a tendency to pass on values which were not quite those of the local society, and that this turned the youth away from the fishing industry. This was considered an important reason for the depopulation of the coastal districts. The so-called Lofoten Project that was initiated in response tried to integrate local material into the curriculum: the students were to learn more about their immediate surroundings, about their parents' trades, the various industries in the local area, local nature and culture, and so on. This research and development project is now history and follow-up and updating may be needed: How are local cultural values presented in today's elementary schools?

An industry in which crises come and go has a communication problem—how to pass on a positive message to the youth? The low interest in fisheries education can hardly be explained in any way other than by the negative impression created by the fishing industry itself. The message about opportunities in the fishing industry is clearly not reaching young folks. "To a great degree, a picture has been drawn of a crisis-ridden industry which may not appear very tempting as a lifetime career," said Bjørn Hersoug, president of the Norwegian College of Fishery Science (*Fiskeribladet* 2 February 1993).

The youth naturally listen to what the adults are talking about, even though what they say is aimed at the authorities. Descriptions of misery may spur the government into action, but they have the opposite effect on young people. It is probably a sign that something is wrong when the province of Finnmark has found it necessary to start classes to "create positive attitudes towards the fishing industry." One would have thought this unnecessary in a province where the children get the fishing industry with their mothers' milk. The project is, of course, worthwhile, but it would have been more helpful if the industry had tried to emphasize the many positive opportunities and not just the problems which will necessarily come and go in an industry in which things can change so rapidly.

INVESTING IN FLEXIBILITY

The heavy investment in the fish processing industry and the gambling on large ocean-going trawlers have created an industry of "mono-cultures." We now have places along the coast which are too specialized and too vulnerable in times of crisis. It does not make it any better that these places are getting fewer and bigger as years go by. Such local societies are vulnerable, and become paralyzed when the fish disappears or the market fails.

An industry which is based on fluctuations as the norm will venture on flexibility, that is, go in the opposite direction. Such an industry will give priority to small enterprises, versatile production and varied market niches. Public statistics show that small firms have survived in recent years while the large units have become fewer and fewer. A policy which promotes flexibility can also maintain a versatile fleet which can carry out various forms of fishing. The fisheries crisis has hit, first and foremost, the boats which caught primarily cod.

A flexible industry would ensure that small places survive and that alternative employment to the fisheries is created. Those families with other work to fall back on have fared better in the crisis than those without it. No longer would attempts be made to eliminate occupational pluralism to promote greater efficiency. In the fjord regions of Troms and Finnmark this is still the only way to survive. A flexible industry would rely on women. Reports indicate that those families which best survived the crisis are those where the women had jobs to go to.

Internationally, the trend is away from standardized mass production and large-scale technology, while handicraft production and small enterprises are experiencing a renaissance. To achieve large plant advantages, small plants form networks, look after common tasks, cooperate on bids and share the production. This is called "flexible specialization" (Piore and Sabel 1984). A policy for a more adaptable fishing industry could harvest knowledge from the organizational forms developed here.

Technical literature (see Nätti 1993) differentiates between "numerical" and "functional" flexibility. In the first, the tendency is for firms to no longer have permanent employees. Instead, people are hired on short-term contracts and are called in when needed and let go when they are no longer needed. "I call, you come," is the principle. Numerical flexibility is much used in the fishing industry and it is not always for the best.

With "functional" flexibility, the person or firm commands a broad spectrum of knowledge and abilities that can be used for many things when needed and has the ability to learn both from their own and others' experience. And now we are back to my previous theme, a theme which has been central all through this book: the need for people with formal education in the industry. Functional flexibility is ensured through a competent management and work force. A fishing industry which takes fluctuations for granted, will be based on flexible production and organizational forms. Such an industry clearly does not take competence for granted, but invests in it.

GOVERNMENT CONTROL

To abandon the idea that it is possible to create perfect control of the fisheries resources and the export market is not to throw up one's hands. Que sera, sera—what will be, will be— has no place in the fishing industry. Adaptation to a changing environment requires different, not necessarily less, management.

For a long time, an issue in the Norwegian fisheries debate has been that plants and workers operate within frameworks which weaken opportunity for realignment and flexibility. Let me present two examples to illustrate this:

Changes in the Fish Export Act were mentioned previously in this book. Until a couple of years ago, plants in the fishing industry were not allowed to export their own products. The Export Act ensured that this important function was looked after by the independent export sector. This reduced the plants' opportunities to exploit their own niches in the market. Above all, it weakened their contacts with the market and thereby the opportunities to learn marketing. The Act has now been amended on that point. This was a step in the right direction for an industry which is investing in flexibility.

Flexibility presumes autonomy; that there is room for local adaptation to variations in the environment. However, experience with the new Export Act, which allows plants to export their own products, indicates that greater local autonomy is not a sufficient prerequisite for increased flexibility. In order for the reforms to produce the desired results, the fish producers must learn the export trade. The challenge is the same here as it is for the fish farmers. The firms must be able to cooperate in marketing to avoid harmful competition. The drop in prices in 1993 on the fresh, salt and dried fish markets in Europe in the wake of the fisheries crisis indicates an acute need for this.

Second example: Present fisheries regulations, with their licensing and quota systems, hamper the fishermen's ability to readjust. They are restricted to the species and operational methods for which they have a quota and licence. This inflexibility in the system encourages the fishermen to fish longer for a particular species of fish than they would have, had they been free to switch to other species. Greater flexibility would have positive effects on both fish populations and fishermen's economy.

Flexibility can be achieved either by the participants being issued quotas/licences for several types of fisheries, or by simply cutting down on the quota and licensing systems. The first would break with the concept of fairness—that the one who has rights in one fishery should manage without rights in another. The second would break fundamentally with the idea behind the existing regulatory system, which is that government intervention is necessary to prevent the tragedy of the commons. But perhaps this is something to think about, nevertheless?

At the international level, researchers are discussing whether quotas for individual stocks are useful (cf. Smith 1991; Finlayson 1991; Wilson and Kleban 1992). The idea behind quota regulations is that by limiting the catching effort, the spawning population will increase, and thereby the possibility of an increased, stable long-term yield. In reality, however, there are many other things which also determine the size of an individual stock, not least the dynamics between various species.

The relationship between cause and effect is thus far too complex for the authorities to learn from what they are doing and thereby fine-tune the regulatory system so that, in the end, it would work accurately, in the short and long term. Data and assessment problems are so great that the authorities are more or less groping in the dark. The argument is that therefore the authorities should take as a starting point a relatively constant biomass, and be open to the idea that the fishermen may switch between species and types of equipment to a greater degree than at present.

WHAT IF?

What if, in the foreseeable future, it became possible to solve the data and assessment problems so that an accurate overview of the eco-systems and the complex interplay between the various populations—including humans as predators—were achieved? What if, some day, full control over the markets and exchange rates were attained? What if one managed to stabilize the operational conditions for those employed in the industry? Would the flexible model then have been so foolish?

Appendix

Table 1 First-hand value, export value, nationally, in 1,000 NOK, percent

	Average 1986-88		1989 %	1990 %	1991 %	1992 %
First-hand value all fish species	5,332,073	(100%)	90	91	105	108*
Export value** All fish species	11,600,163	(100%)	102	111	124	125
Export value** cod	2,816,489	(100%)	80	74	101	129

* Interim figures from the Fisheries Directorate, not deflated.
** Deflated.

Source: *Fiskarkalender* (Lauritzen 1993), Norut Samfunnsforskning A/S.

Table 2 Catch value in 1,000 NOK and amount, tonnes, percent. Not deflated

	Average 1986-88		1989 %	1990 %	1991 %	1992 %
Cod						
Finnmark	433,180	(100%)	68	67	106	174
excl. foreign supplies				45	90	75
Troms	384,813	(100%)	74	53	107	129
excl. foreign supplies				49	78	87
Nordland	538,541	(100%)	71	77	119	135
excl. foreign supplies					119	134
All species of fish						
Finnmark	849,467	(100%)	69	75	93	129
excl. foreign supplies				62	68	70
Troms	765,488	(100%)	94	84	111	123
excl. foreign supplies				82	96	98
Nordland	791,769	(100%)	73	86	124	125
excl. foreign supplies					123	123
South Norway	2,925,349	(100%)	99	99	101	93*
Amount of raw material—all species of fish**						
Finnmark	102,039	(100%)	68	40	69	75
Troms	66,052	(100%)	103	55	99	110
Nordland	91,231	(100%)	81	76	125	138

* Interim figures from the Fisheries Directorate.
** Foreign supplies not included.

Source: Norwegian Raw Fish Association, Fish Calendar, Norwegian Fishermen's Association (Norges Råfisklag, Fiskerikalender, Norges Fiskarlag).

Table 3 Percentage increase in first time distraint auctions on loans from the Housing Bank

	Average 1986–1988	1989 %	1990 %	1991 %	1992 %
Nord-Troms and Finnmark	207 (100%)	182	191	136	101
Fishing Municipalities rest of Troms and Nordland	142 (100%)	110	142	94	115

* Includes Karlsøy. Figures for fishing municipalities are not available.

Source: The Housing Bank.

Table 4 The Fishermen's Bank: Distraint auctions and takeovers of mortgages, vessels, plants

	Average 1985–1987	1988 %	1989 %	1990 %	1991 %	1992 %
North Norway and North Trøndelag						
- Vessels	22 (100%)	205	291	295	141	141
- Plants	3 (100%)	166	733	366	500	633
South Norway						
- Vessels	10 (100%)	210	290	370	110	140
- Plants	0 (100%)	200(2)	100(1)	300(3)	100(1)	0

Source: The Fishermen's Bank.

Table 5 Registered fishermen with fishing as main trade*. Percent

	Average no. of fishermen, 1985–1988	1989 %	1990 %	1991 %	1992 %
Finnmark	2,295 (100%)	95	87	84	83
Troms	3,802 (100%)	96	90	88	86
Nordland	5,275 (100%)	94	89	86	86
South Norway	11,057 (100%)	96	94	93	91

* All municipalities.

Source: Fisheries Directorate: Fishermen Census (Fiskeridirektoratet: Fiskarmantallet).

Table 6 Unemployed in percent, by number of registered workers in Norwegian fishing municipalities, 1986–1990

Unemployed	Average 1986-88	1989	1990
Fishing municipalities:			
Finnmark	8.8	15.8	22.9
Troms	7.7	12.3	11.5
Nordland	6.9	10.5	13.0
South Norway	3.9	7.4	8.8
All fishing municipalities	6.0	10.4	12.4
All types of municipalities:			
North Norway	6.7	10.5	11.0
South Norway	3.2	5.8	6.4
Nationally	3.9	6.7	7.4

Source: Norwegian Social Science Data Services (Norsk samfunnsvitenskapelig datatjeneste).

Table 7 Net migration (outmigration—inmigration). Norwegian fishing municipalities. Percent

	Average net migration 1986–1988		1989 %	1990 %	1991 %
North Norway:					
Finnmark	234	(100%)	38	85	77
Troms	263	(100%)	67	61	44
Nordland	367	(100%)	83	54	49
South Norway	115	(100%)	165	403	170
Nationally	979	(100%)	77	96	56

Source: Norwegian Social Science Data Services (Norsk samfunnsvitenskapelig datatjeneste).

Notes

Preface

1. The Coastal Expertise Committee (Kystkompetanseutvalget) was established in 1985 at the initiative of the National Association of the Fish Processing Industry, the Fish Processing Industry Employers' Association/NAF, the Norwegian Food and Allied Workers Union/LO (National Labour Organization) and the Management Training Council for Norway. The Committee's mandate was to set up an action plan for management development in the fish processing industry.

The Committee has worked closely with the Department of Fisheries. The Department of Culture and Science has also been involved and has been kept informed about the work. The Institute for Fisheries Sciences at the University of Tromsø carried out an extensive management study in connection with the Committee's survey. The Committee's work is financed by the Departments of Fisheries, Municipal Affairs and Labour.

The Management Training Council of Norway is the body responsible for the Committee's work and presentations.

Professor Svein Jentoft, was responsible for the Committee's survey and analysis of the management situation in the contemporary fish processing industry. He also participated in most of the Committee meetings.

The Committee's Mandate

The Committee's mandate was established with the approval of the organizations and departments concerned:

1. To assess the need for management at various levels in the Norwegian fish processing industry based on a 15-year development perspective. The perspective will require an evaluation of assumed future structure and of assumed future tasks in the Norwegian fish processing industry.

2. To survey management qualifications in the contemporary fish processing industry.

3. Based on the above, to assess the need for:

(a) further training of the present managers

(b) special measures for new recruitment into management

(c) coordination of training programmes with particular emphasis on management tasks/positions in the fish processing industry.

4. Propose the structuring of special measures for management development in the fish processing industry.

During its work, the Committee should hold meetings with representatives of industry, research and education, as well as industrial organizations, to ensure the broadest possible participation in, and support of, the further work in developing management in the industry.

In its work the Committee has found that it is both difficult and inadvisable to discuss management development and expertise requirements with a limited part of the industry in isolation. Therefore, the Committee has also suggested a continuation of its work where management and realignment expertise in the entire fishing industry would be discussed as a package. In this presentation, we have limited the scope to production on shore, the so-called fish processing industry. Fishing and mariculture are only touched on to the extent that these parts of the industry relate to the industry's sphere of activity.

Chapter 1

1. This particular fishery takes place from January until late March as the mature cod comes down from the Barents Sea to spawn in Lofoten, a string of islands on the coast of Northern Norway. The Lofoten fishery has been called the biggest cod fishery in the world. It used to attract up to 30,000 fishermen for the season from all over the coast. Economically, the Lofoten fishery still is important even though the number of participating fishermen has declined to approximately 4,000 in 1990. This number reflects the general reduction in the number of fishermen in Norway since World War II (from 115,000 in 1946 to 25,000 in 1992).

2. In the debate, which was covered widely by the media, Mr. Munkejord characterised the argument of his opponents in ways that were considered unusual and improper for a minister of the government.

3. Unlike Canada, Norway is not a federal state. Provinces (fylke) in the Norwegian system do not have the autonomy or resources of Canadian provinces, for instance fish processing is generally a provincial matter in Canada whereas it is a national concern in Norway.

4. From *Trumpet of Nordland* by Petter Dass (1647–1708) Norwegian poet priest. First published in 1735.

Chapter 2

1. In Norway, a municipality (kommune) is a geographically delineated area with a council elected by the local population. These councils are responsible for such matters as schools, health and social services, industrial development, local transportation and culture. Many of their responsibilities are delegated to it by the central government, while others are matters of purely local concern. The municipalities finance their activities partly through transfer payments from the central government, partly through taxation of its own population and partly through duties and fees for municipal services. Norwegian municipalities have more extensive responsibilities than Canadian municipalities. The expenditure of Norwegian municipalities as a percentage of the gross national product is about double that of Canadian municipalities. (Fevolden *et al.*, 1992). There are a total of 439 municipalities in Norway, 40 of which are classified by the Central (Norwegian) Bureau of Statistics as fishing municipalities.

2. As one of the successful welfare states in Europe, Norway has been used to unemployment rates of less than 5 percent since World War II.

3. Many visiting fishermen from other parts of the coast prefer to use their quotas during the Lofoten fisheries when the prices are at their highest.

4. Norway borders Russia in the north. Finnmark province lies partly adjacent to Russia.

Chapter 3

1. Ragnvaldur Hannesson (1990) has calculated that the potential resource rent from Norwegian fisheries is at about 2.076 billion Norwegian kroner.

2. A committee formed by members of the three provincial parliaments (ting) of the provinces that form Northern Norway, including the district of Nordalen in North Trøndelag.

3. The Fishery Conservation and Management Act—also called the Magnuson Act—was passed in 1976. It specifies that any fishing effort placed on the resources must be conducted at an "optimum yield" (OY) level.

   OY is defined as the biological concept of MSY "as modified by any relevant economic, social, or ecological factor." The way to ensure that such factors are taken into consideration in the regulatory decision-making process, is a system of public participation. Public input comes from various interest groups that form the Regional Management Councils, there are eight such councils in the U.S.A.

Chapter 4

1. As a comparison, Liv Schjelderup (1980), in a study of small enterprises in the workshop industry, found that 39 percent of the managers were involved in such work every day.

2. Until 1991 it was generally illegal to export fish without a special licence, and the issuing of licences was largely controlled by organizations of exporters. This system often prevented processors from integrating "downstream," that is, becoming exporters of their own products. The Fish Export Act of 1990 reversed the principle: Export is free unless the government decides that exceptions are needed. Those who now want to become exporters only need to register with the Fisheries Export Council and pay a fee of 15,000 kr. ($3,000 Cdn.).

3. The Raw Fish Act, enacted in 1938, gives the fishermen's cooperative sales organizations the authority to fix minimum prices, which the fish buyers have to accept if they want to stay in business. Processors are not allowed to purchase fish from outside these channels and the organizations also decide if a plant will be given permission to act as buyers or not. Thus the Raw Fish Act gives the fishermen, through their sales organizations, a monopoly on the sale of raw fish. A central reason for introducing the Raw Fish Act was to regulate income distribution. By setting minimum prices on the raw fish, the Act also forced processors and exporters to obtain the best prices possible from the market. The Act was thus also a device for creating higher profitability in the fishing industry as a whole.

Chapter 6

1. The OIF projects are training measures in the fish processing industry (opplæringstiltak i fiskeindustrien).

Chapter 7

1. The project was financed by the Norwegian Fisheries Research Council of Norway (Norges Fiskeriforsknings-råd).

Chapter 8

1. There has been a long standing public policy in Norway to maintain a decentralized settlement structure.

2. It must be admitted that the Fisherman's Census (Fiskarmantallet) is not the most reliable base for statistical analysis. People have a tendency to appear in the census for some time after they have stopped fishing. The year 1983 was selected, however, because that year there was a considerable tightening up of the recording procedures. If it is possible to assume that the records are about equally inaccurate in all municipalities, then the problem is not so great as far as our conclusion is concerned.

3. In some fishing municipalities there have been experiments with organizing a system of relief crewing so that fishermen could have more time with their families even during the peak season.

Chapter 9

1. In Norway, daycare workers are unionized.

Chapter 10

1. They may be concerned about the oversupply at a national level, but they tend to ignore the problem on the local level.

Chapter 11

1 According to *Dagbladet* 18 January 1990, he answered: "I've got enough to do raising my own children, I shouldn't have to raise yours too." He later apologized to her.

Chapter 12

1. Skippers take turns crewing each other's boats, thus reducing crew costs.

Chapter 13

1. Black fisheries in Norway means unreported fishing above the quota.
2. Since the late 1960s Norway has had a so called "Main Agreement" under which the Fishermen's Association negotiates subsidies on behalf of the entire industry. The subsidies were originally intended to improve the efficiency of the industry. However, the system was not successful in its primary aim. Rather, it has quite perversely become a series of grants to large-scale operations particularly in South Norway (see Jentoft and Mikalsen 1987).
3. This organization was established in 1988, and was initiated by a group of fishermen in the Lofoten district, in frustration over what they saw as an off-shore large scale fisheries bias of the Norwegian Fishermen's Association (established 1926).
4. See Chapter 4, Note 3.
5. In an article, I have summed up the international experience with cooperative regulatory forms in the fisheries (Jentoft 1989).

Chapter 15

1. This is probably what makes the politicians, as soon as they get into responsible positions, declare that there is no such thing as a north-south conflict.
2. A government appointed task force, the so called Moxnes Committee, suggested that fishermen's sales organizations should no longer have the authority to license buyers of raw fish. The committee presented its report in 1990, but its proposals have not yet been implemented (NOU 1990:24).
3. The press release by the Norwegian Coastal Fishermen's Association (Norges Kystfiskarlag) is dated 7 June 1991.
4. The statement concerning the fish-farming industry originated with secretary-general Paul Birger Torgness, to the newspaper *Nordlys* (3 June 1991).

References

Apostle, Richard and Svein Jentoft 1991 "Nova Scotia and North Norway Fisheries: The Future of Small Scale Processors." *Marine Policy*, March, pp. 110–110.

Arntzen, Ann Helene 1989 "Turistmagneten" og den kommersielle fantasi." *Tidsskriftet Ottar*, Nr. 2. Tromsø Museum.

Barnes, J.A. 1954 "Class and Committees in a Norwegian Island Parish." *Human Relations*, VII(1). February.

Bjørgo-utvalget (The Bjørgo Committee) 1990 *Nybrott og gjenreisning: Ny kunnskapspolitikk for Nord Norge*. NAVF: Norges Allmennvitenskapelig forskningsråd.

Boulding, Kenneth 1977 "Commons and Community: The Idea of a Public." In G. Hardin & J. Baden (eds.), *Managing the Commons*. San Francisco: W.H. Freeman and Company.

Brinchmann, Knut and Øystein Jensen 1990 *Turistproduktet Nord Norge*. Arbeidsnotat Nr. 1056/90, Nordlandsforskning.

Brochmann, Bjørn 1981 "Virkninger på lang sikt av statsstøtte til fiskeriene." *Sosialøkonomen*, nr. 2.

Brox, Ottar 1984 *Nord Norge—Fra allmenning til koloni*. Universitetsforlaget.

Bruntland Commission (Brundtlandskommisjonen) 1987 "Vår felles framtid." Rapport fra Verdenskommisjonen for miljø og utvikling. Tiden Norsk Forlag.

Coastal Expertise Committee, The (Kystkompetanseutvalget) 1990 *Fra primærnæring til marin næringsmiddelindustri: Handlingsplan for ledelses—og kompetanseutvikling i norsk fiskerinæring*. Lederopplærings rådet/Fiskeridepartementet.

Cohen, Anthony P. 1985 *The Symbolic Construction of Community*. London: Tavistock Publications.

Copes, Parzival 1986 "A Critical Review of the Individual Quota as a Device in Fisheries Management." *Land Economics*, 62(3):278–291.

Dahl-Jacobsen, Knut 1965 "Informasjonstilgang og likebehandling i den offentlige virksomhet." *Tidsskrift for samfunnsforskning*, nr. 2.

Dalså, Adrian 1987 *Innføring av ny teknologi: EDB i fiskeindustrien på Island, Færøyene og i Nord Norge. En sammenlikning av konsekvenser.* Kandidatsoppgave, Institutt for fiskerfag, Universitetet i Tromsø.

Didriksen, Johnny, 1990 "Det var mye å leve for, men lite å leve av—Om pionertiden i norsk fiskeoppdrett." In P. Holm, S. Jentoft and B. Steene (eds.), *Norsk oppdrettsnæring ved inngangen til 90-åra.* Vedlegg til handlingsplan fra Kystkompetanseutvalget. Lederopplæringsrådet/ Fiskeridepartementet.

Fevolden, Trond, Terje P. Hagen and Rune Sørensen 1992 *Kommunal organisering. Styring, effectivitet og demokrati.* Tano Forlag.

Finlayson, Chris 1991 "Notes on Chaos in Fisheries Management by Estellie Smith." *Maritime Anthropological Studies*, 4(1):91–97.

Flakstad, Anne Grethe 1987 "Befolkningsutvikling i et tokjønnet perspektiv—en annerledes historie?" *Sosiologi i idag.* Nr. 5/6.

Flåten, Ola 1990 "Økonomi og flerbestandsforvaltning." *The Seminary report: Flerbestandsforvaltning. Et Barentshav av muligheter.* Fiskerikandidatenes Forening/Norges Fiskerihøgskole.

Førsund, Finn, Erling Holmøy, Ole-Jørgen Mørkved, Victor D. Norman and Rune Sørensen 1991 *Mot bedre vitende? Effektiviseringsmuligheter i offentlig virksomhet.* Stiftelsen for samfunns—og næringslivsforskning. Norges Handelshøyskole.

Foss, Lene 1989 "Nettverk og entreprenørskap. Teoretisk perspektiv og empirisk tilnærming." *Arbeidsnotat*, nr. 24. Senter for anvendt forskning. Norges Handelshøyskole.

Gerrard, Siri 1983 "Kvinner i fiskeridistrikter—fiskerinæringas 'bakkemannskap.'" In B. Hersoug (ed.), *Kan fiskerinæringa styres?* Novus Forlag.

Gordon, H. Scott 1954 "The Economic Theory of Common Property Resource." *Journal of Political Economy*, 62, April.

Granovetter, Mark 1985 "Economic Action and Social Structure: The problem of Embeddedness." *American Journal of Sociology*, 91(3):481–510.

_____ 1973 "The Strength of Weak Ties." *American Journal of Sociology*, 78(6)1360–1378.

Hallenstvedt, Abraham 1990 "Organisering av ansvar." In Yngvar Løchen (ed.), *Formål og fellesskap.* Projektet Alternativ Framtid, Oslo.

_____ 1982 *Med lov og organisasjon: organisering av interesser og markeder i norsk fiskerinæring.* Universitetsforlaget.

Hannesson, Ragnvaldur 1980 *En samfunnsøkonomisk lønnsom fiskerinæring: Struktur, gevinst, forvaltning.* Rapport utarbeidet for Administrasjons—og arbeidsdepartementet.

Hardin, Garret 1968 "The Tragedy of the Commons." *Science*, 162:1243–1248.

Henriksen, Jan 1990 *Fra erfaring til organisasjonslæring. En studie av læringsatferd og kompetanseutvikling i norsk fiskeindustri.* Hovedoppgave, Universitetet i Tromsø: Institutt for samfunnsvitenskap.

Hersoug, Bjørn 1985 *Fiskernes vandring—Om yrkesskifte og mobilitet blandt norske fiskere, 1971–80.* Stensilserie D, nr. 1, Norges Fiskerihøgskole.

_____ and Alf H. Hoel 1991 *Hvem tok fisken?* Notat: Norges Fiskerihøgskole.

_____ 1990 *Privatisering eller regionalisering.* Notat: Norges Fiskerihøgskole.

Holm, Petter, Svein Jentoft and Bardon Steene (eds.) 1990 *Norsk oppdrettsnæring ved inngangen til 90-åra. Vedlegg til handlingsplanen fra Kystkompetanseutvalget.* Lederopplæringsrådet/Fiskeridepartementet.

Husmo, Marit and Eva Munk-Madsen 1989 *Kjønnsmyter med konsekvenser: En analyse av skillet mellom kvinner og menn i industriell fiskeforedling til lands og til vanns.* Projektnotat: Norges Fiskerihøgskole.

Jacobsen, Knut Dahl 1965 "Informasjonstilgang og likebehandling i den offentlige virksomhet." *Tidsskrift for samfunnsforskning* nr. 2, pp. 147–160.

Jacobsen, Jens Kristian 1989 "Før reisen fantes oppdagelsen, etter reisen finnes turismen." *Tidsskriftet Ottar*, nr. 2. Tromsø Museum.

Jentoft, Svein 1990 *Organisasjon og ledelse i nord-norsk fiskeindustri. Vedlegg til Handlingsplan for lederutvikling i fiskeindustrien.* Lederopplæringsrådet/Fiskeridepartementet.

_____ 1989 "Fisheries co-management: Delegating Government Responsibility to Fishermen's Organizations." *Marine Policy*, April, pp. 137–154.

_____ (ed.) 1989 *Mor til rors: Organisering av dagligliv og yrkesaktivitet i fiskerfamilier.* Norges Fiskerihøgskole.

_____ 1987 "Allmenningens tragedie—statens ansvar?" *Tidsskrift for Samfunnsforskning*, bd. 28, 369–390.

_____ 1984 "Hvor sårbare er fiskerimiljøene." In S. Jentoft and C. Wadel (eds.), *I samme båt: Lokale sysselsettingssystemer i fiskerinæringen.* Universitetsforlaget.

_____ and Trond Kristoffersen 1989 "Fishermen's co-management: The case in the Lofoten Fishery." *Human Organization*, 48(4):355–365.

_____ and Knut H. Mikalsen 1987 "Government Subsidies in the Norwegian Fisheries: Regional Development or Political Favouritism?" *Marine Policy*, July 1987, pp. 217–228.

_____and Cato Wadel (eds.) 1984 *I samme båt: Lokale sysselsetting-ssystemer i fiskerinæringen.* Universitetsforlaget.

Jervan, Bård, Knut Sevaldsen, Rolf Akselsen and Knud H. Staugaard 1986 *1000 nye årsverk i det ferie- og fritidsbetingede reiselivet i Nord Norge.* Reiselivsutvikling A/S, Oslo.

Kamfjord, Georg 1990 *Den Norske Kultur og Miljøpark: Utviklingsstrategier for OL-Norge.* Lillehammer Olympia Vekst A/S.

Kristiansen, Aslak 1985 *Har vi råd til et effektivt fiskerioppsyn?* Projektnotat: Norges Fiskerihøgskole.

MacDonald, Don 1988 *Bedriftsorganisasjonens logikk: Fra klassisk linje til organisk mikroenhet.* Tano Forlag.

MacInnes, Daniel, Svein Jentoft and Anthony Davis (eds.) 1991 *Social Research and Public Policy Formation in the Fisheries: Norwegian and Canadian Experiences.* Dalhousie University, Nova Scotia: Institute of Oceans.

March, James G. and Johan P. Olsen 1989 *Rediscovering Institutions: The Organizational Basis of Politics.* New York: The Free Press.

McCay, Bonnie J. 1984 "The Pirates of the Piscary: Ethnology of Illegal Fishing in New Jersey." *Ethnology*, 31(1):17–37.

McGoodwin, James R. 1990 *Crisis in the World's Fisheries: People, Problems and Politics.* Stanford, Ca.: Stanford University Press.

Midré, Georges and Anne Solberg 1980 "Sosial integrasjon og sosial kontrol." In I.L. Høst and C. Wadel (eds.), *Fiske og lokalsamfunn.* Universitetsforlaget.

Munk-Madsen, Eva 1990 "Skibet er ladet med køn: En analyse af kønsrelationer og kvinders vilkår i fabrikskibsflåden." Norges Fiskerihøgskole.

Myhra, Hans Ludvik and Leif Langli 1988 *Erfaringslæring som verktøy i bedriftsutvikling.* Statens Yrkespedagogiske høyskole.

Nadel-Klein, Jane and Dona Lee Davis (eds.) 1988 *To Work and to Weep: Women in Fishing Economies.* St. John's, Memorial University of Newfoundland: Institute of Social and Economic Research.

Nilsen, Ragnar 1987 *Befolkningsutvikling, flytting og rekruttering i Nord-Norge. Oppsummering av resultat fra befolkningsprosjektet.* FORUT: Forskningsstiftelsen ved Universitetet i Tromsø.

NordREFO 1987 *Regionalpolitik i en nätverksekonomi—en seminarierapport.* Rapport nr. 4, Nordiska Institutet for regionalpolitisk forskning. Helsinki, Finland.

NOU 1980:22 *Arbeidstid i fiske.*

_____ 1982:5 *Råstoffutjevning i fiskeindustrien.*

_____ 1984:21A *Statlig næringsstøtte i distriktene.*

_____ 1990:24 *Fiske industriens organisering og rammevilkår.*

Nätti, Jauko 1993 "Atypical Employment in the Nordic Countries: Towards Marginalization or Normalization?" In Thomes B. Boje and Sven E. Olsson (eds.), Oslo: Universitetsforlaget, (forthcoming).

Olsen, Berit 1990 "Hva skal vi gjøre med depresjonen på kysten?" *Sosial trygd,* 12:24–8.

Parliamentary Report (St. meld. nr. 29) 1988–89 *Politikk for regional utvikling.*

_____ 1988–89 (St. meld. nr. 46) *Miljø og utvikling.* Norges oppfølging av Verdenskommisjonens rapport.

_____ 1990–1991 (St. meld. nr. 32) *På rett kjøl: Om kystens utviklingsmuligheter.*

Piore, Michael J. and Charles F. Sabel 1984 *The Second Industrial Divide: Possibilities for Prosperity.* New York: Basic Books.

Randa, Svein and Jan Aslaksen 1991 *Vinterloddefisket 1991: En analyse av loddenæringa under vinterloddefisket 1991.* Utbyggingsfondet i. Finnmark: Vadsø.

Regional Committee for Nord Norge and Namdalen (Landsdelsutvalget) 1991 *Ny resurspolitikk—innsatsregulering i fiske.* Bodø.

Rossvær, Viggo 1989 "Fiskerkvinneaksjon på Sørøya—Innenfraforståelse og utenfraforståelse." *Tidsskriftet Albatross,* nr. 1.

Saugestad, Sidsel 1988 *Partners in Enterprise: The Social Organization of Paid and Unpaid Labour. Case Studies of Household Viability in Northern Norway.* Universitetet i Tromsø: Institutt for samfunnsvitenskap.

Schjelderup, Liv 1980 *Småforetak i en stordriftssamfunn.* Universitetsforlaget.

Schumpeter, Joseph A. 1943/1979 *Capitalism, Socialism and Democracy.* George Allen & Unwin Ltd.

Seierstad, Ståle, Bjørn Sagdahl and Audun Sandberg 1985 *Kystsamfunn på kår: Nord-Norge som oljeprovins.* Universitetsforlaget.

Smith, M. Estellie 1991 "Chaos in Fisheries Management." *Maritime Anthropological Studies,* 5(1):67–75.

Solheim, Jorun, Hanne Heen and Øystein G. Holter 1986 *Nordsjøliv og hjemmeliv. Part I and II.* Rapport nr. 35. Oslo: Arbeidsforskningsinstituttet.

Steinmetz, L.L. 1969 "Critical Stages of Small Business Growth." *The Business Horizon.* February.

Sundt, Eilert 1975 *Haram—et eksempel fra fiskeridistriktene (1859).* Verker i utvalg 3. Gyldendal Norsk Forlag.

Thiessen, Victor, Anthony Davis and Svein Jentoft 1991 *The Veiled Crew. An exploratory study of wives' reported and desired contributions to coastal fisheries enterprises in Northern Norway and Nova Scotia.* Universitetet i Tromsø: Institutt for samfunnsvitenskap.

Viken, Arvid 1989 *The Nordkapp Sky-line: Nordkapp sett med turistøyne.* FDH-rapport nr. 7. Finnmark Distrikts-høgskole.

Weil, Frederick D. 1989 "The Sources and Structure of Legitimation in Wester Democracies: A consolidated model tested with time-series data in six countries since the Second World War." *American Sociological Review,* October, pp. 682–706.

Wilson, James A. and Peter Kleban 1992 "Practical Implications of Chaos in Fisheries: Ecologically Adopted Management." *Maritime Anthropological Studies,* 5(1):67–75.

Østerud, Øivind 1979 *Det planlagte samfunn: Om sentral-planleggingens fremvekst og grenser.* Gyldendal Norsk Forlag.

Index

ISER BOOKS

Studies

Mailing Address:
ISER Books (Institute of Social and Economic Research)
Memorial University of Newfoundland
St. John's, Newfoundland, Canada, A1C 5S7

PRINTED IN CANADA